Practical HOUSES

FOR

Contemporary LIVING

by

JEAN GRAF

DON GRAF, A.I.A.

F. W. Dodge Corporation, New York

Foreword

This is a book about personal desires . . . and houses that satisfy them.

These are desires for living the best possible way, within the framework of conditions.

First is the dream, big or small. Sometimes the dream must bow to reality. Otherwise a house could never be.

The conditions that give shape to the dream may be those of location or budget or family or impulse.

The solution of all these is a successful house.

Jean and Don Graf

Contents

Chapter heading illustrations by Lowell Hess.

Successful Houses Fit People

This book is a collection of stories about contented owners. Each house is as individual as the people who live in it—for each is a successful working out of particular problems of site and budget and taste.

Ingenuity, hard-headed practicality and a fine regard for the personal element characterize these houses—rather than adherence to a "style" such as Colonial or Modern. A house can no more be poured into a mold than can a person.

As similar beings, we agree on one basic thing —our comfort requirements. We all get too hot or too cold at about the same temperatures. We all wash and sleep and eat, and get wet when the roof leaks. Products that increase comfort or save work are mass-produced for a national— and very receptive—market. The same dishwasher will work just as well in California as in Vermont; the same house, if expected to deliver the same comfort, will not.

One region, one piece of land is like no other. A house must be accommodated to the weather, the slopes, the view, the neighbors. Size and layout depends upon X number of children, X number of expected company, X number of help-hours, from once-a-week baby sitter to resident cook. Even these practical differences could be charted so we might arrive at a series of "standard" houses, except for one factor—the human being who is to live in it.

"VIVE LA DIFFÉRENCE!"

A house should be a place to feel at home— whether "at home" means dining with candles, working a power saw, cooking a salt steak, painting with oils, playing with the children, or just getting away from it all. The way a house looks and acts should reflect personal enthusiasms and efforts. The successful house bears the stamp of its owner.

How to go about having one? Look first to yourself with honest introspection, and be willing to separate valid desires from superficial ideas. With building costs high, there is no room for waste in a house, but there is always a place for sentiment. Look secondly to your architect, a kind of Renaissance man, partly engineer, artist, expediter, psycho-analyst and businessman. Specify results within your budget. He will devise the means. Argue with him creatively.

HOW TO READ BOOK, PLANS

This is planned as a "working" book, one to be read and re-read, kept handy for reference. Consider the first run-through as an excursion in taste, then study pages more closely with an eye to your own problems.

The individual stories of owners and how they achieved their successful houses cover a wide range in price, geography, taste and way of life. Among them, you will find conditions that match yours—in no single house, perhaps, but in a combination of several.

The book is divided roughly into three parts, each based on the *leading* requirement that governed design of the separate houses. These are Size of Family (first three sections), Location, (next two) and Sheer Desire (the last). This is a headline grouping at best, as every house in the book represents a balance of all three.

To help pin-point answers to specific questions, a Concordance in the back lists everything from "built-in headboards" to "houses on lakes," and where to find examples in the individual stories.

Short of an actual visit to a home, the only way to get the feel of a house and how it works is to read plans and photographs and copy *together*. Spend some time on the plans, which have been simplified for easy reading. Each one is drawn to the same scale (1/16 inch to a foot) to enable accurate comparison of floor areas. Each plan is so placed on the page that the main entrance is at the bottom of the sketch. Imagine yourself in the house, walking from room to room, from indoors to outdoors, looking through the windows.

The plan shows the whole. The photographs show significant parts. Numbered arrows indicate the camera views and are keyed to each picture. If you turn the book this way and that to relate a picture to the plan, then you are really "reading" the house.

A house is supposed to have three dimensions. It has a fourth, cost. Unless a house is within an owner's means, it can never be built at all. Sometimes finished details and decor are sacrificed for ample space. Sometimes a tiny house has its space planned for double or triple duty, and furnishings reflect this. Sometimes an unconventional construction device is money-saving. Read the story behind the house to know whether it was meant to be lush or lean.

Planning a house is like playing tug-of-war with an octopus. At first, it seems as though all the various demands of space and site and private desires and building commissioners and bankers could never be resolved. But they always are. A good trick is to arm yourself with two lists—one for all the things you want, and one for what you could really do without.

TWO WISE MEN SAID:

"When we mean to build
We first survey the plot, then draw the model;
And when we see the figures of the house,
Then must we rate the cost of the erection;
Which if we find outweighs ability,
What do we then, but draw anew the model
In fewer offices; or at least
Desist to build at all."

Shakespeare, King Henry IV

"For which of you, desiring to build a tower, does not first sit down and count the cost, whether he has enough to complete it? Otherwise, when he has laid a foundation, and is not able to finish, all who see it begin to mock him, saying, 'This man began to build, and was not able to finish.'"

Luke 14: 28, 29 (Revised Standard Version)

Don't let these sentiments discourage you. The least expensive part of a house, and the most valuable is thoughtful planning. Add a patient heart, an open mind, a sense of humor—and the house that results can be very truly yours.

vii.

WHERE YOU LIVE

Deep in the pines on Mt. Desert Is., Maine, the Garrity house has pitched roof to shed snow, maximum windows to catch light, view. Natural pine, inside and out, echoes rustic location. Architect: Ambrose Higgins.

Spectacular desert setting in Phoenix, Arizona. Wide overhangs cut hot sun. Exterior is of cool-looking, heat-resisting pumice block, popular in this area. Owners: The J. C. Garretts. Architect: Fred M. Guirey.

Split level house on a Minnesota hill. Low winter sun ducks under overhang, which prevents sky glare in summer. Natural fieldstone on exterior. Owners: The H. F. Shedds. Architects: Thorshov and Cerny.

MAKES A DIFFERENCE—IN MATERIALS AND DESIGN

Location affects the cost, function and flavor of a house. Before a desire for a certain type of structure becomes a conviction, take a calculating look around your area.

Building materials are heavy. Their price at point of origin or manufacture increases the farther they are shipped, the more they are handled. Redwood is native to California and is commonly used there for exteriors. By the time it reaches the Atlantic Coast, it becomes a luxury material. Fieldstone is something to stumble over in New England. It is worth its weight in beefsteaks in Kansas.

Cost favors the local material, and gradually a region develops a "look" of its own. With the persistent use of a material come the men who know how to use it—so that there are more skilled brick layers in Missouri than in Maine. It is only good sense to take advantage of local materials and workmanship, whatever your choice of design.

Climate shapes a house. Deep-rooted differences in regional design could be plotted on a weather map. Thick adobe walls became a characteristic of desert houses, not only because clay was handy, but because of its cooling effect. Land-hugging low houses resisted the sweeping winds of the plains. Steeply pitched roofs shed heavy snow loads. Central chimneys with their fireplaces warmed the rooms around them, and dictated the plan. These practical solutions, devised by early builders, mellowed into a local heritage of design.

Contemporary design is shaped just as surely by the matching of men's wits against the climate. No function of a house is being given greater attention today than the control of heat and cold, air movement and humidity. New products open up new possibilities, even as the perfection of double glazing permitted the use of window-walls in cold climates. New products spark new ways to use them.

Honest modern design is no matter of whim, even though the results may look unfamiliar. The width of a roof overhang, the way a house faces, a compact or rambling plan of a house may depend upon the sun or lack of it, or the way the wind and rain blows. With building costs important, a modern architect tries to figure the greatest comfort for the lowest price. This applies not only to the original cost, but cost of maintenance, too.

The more climate to combat, the more protection must be built into a house. In the North, more insulation, larger heating systems, sturdier construction. In the sultry part of the South,

A den with no windows. Owner, Terry Turner, rides the flat plains around Colby, Kansas, where a limitless view and swirling dust make him relish a retreat that is completely closed in. Architect: Victor Hornbein.

ix.

Colonial is preferred in South Carolina, and the house below with its shuttered windows looks quite proper from the street. At left is rear view, showing the influence of the ranch-type plan, and modern awning windows for ventilation. Architect-owner: W. E. Freeman, Jr.

X.

louvers to trap reluctant breezes, air-conditioning, insulation against the sun.

Where weather is equable year-round, structures can be small, patios ample. Where outdoor living is seasonal and unpredictable, houses must be larger to meet equivalent needs. Thus, there are more basements and attached garages in Michigan, more flat-slab foundations and carports in California. A sweet little ranch-house, advertised at $10,000 in Palo Alto, could cost twice that in Poughkeepsie.

A third factor influences the rightness of a house in an area—and that is the flavor of the locale. Besides the economics and climate just mentioned, it is the people who lived there and added a bit of themselves to their setting. It is

history made tangible in old houses still standing —or their copies. Overtones in design may be Spanish or French or English or Dutch or 20th Century American. This distillation of history can add up to a charming heritage—or a bad habit. Like choice aged cheese, the older the region, the stronger the flavor of history.

To lift an old house out of the context of its times, and copy it slavishly, is to create a museum piece for yourself. Not a place in which to live. But the best ideas creamed from the past can enrich the present. A hooked rug can look handsome on a radiant heated floor.

Whether you decide to adopt or reject the historic flavor of a locality may not be entirely up to you. In cities and suburbs, zoning laws often specify the size of house, number of stories, choice of materials. In one section of Buffalo, "ranch houses" are designed with a story-and-a-half, to get around the law against one-story houses, enacted to control the rash of bargain bungalows in the 1920's.

Limitations on style may be written into a deed, when a developer wants to create a local "flavor" artificially, or a community wants to preserve a proud ancestry. Bankers are notoriously conservative, and tend to lend on designs that "look safe," because they have been around for a while. You might remind them that they are betting on futures as you are, and the resale value of a house ten years hence is important.

Riding a trend is like buying stock on the way up. Trends in building are not fads. They emerge slowly as the sum of good results for individual owners, the impact of new materials, and broad changes in social behavior. One region may respond to them more quickly than another.

Underlying the personal and local differences in the houses shown, note features of planning that occur frequently, and key today's trend:

1) Service and main entrances sharing the same driveway. Location of kitchen, utility room and garage on street side, or "front."

2) Utilization of entire plot. With rear area freed of service, it can become a private, pleasant focus of entire house. Some houses embrace this area with twin wings.

3) Sagacious use of windows. Minimal against neighbors or street or weather, floor-to-ceiling with a reason.

4) One-story houses, mostly basementless for one-level traffic. Flat roofs that permit free arrangement of living spaces beneath. Where land or living needs call for it, the use of split levels requiring only a few steps up or down, rather than a flight.

5) The canny location of storage facilities at point of use. Specially designed storage.

6) The isolation of bedrooms from household operation.

7) Built-in self-sufficiency, and pride in the parts of the house that work. A new companionship between kitchen and living areas.

Today's house has a bigger-than-ever job to do —on a 24-hour duty. More people are building for retirement, working at home in their professions, enjoying creative play, keeping house without help, than ever before. If a house cannot serve a life, in a manner that befits the 1950's, it has no business being built today.

A private, country location encourages free spirit in design. In the J. T. Kelly house, Barrington, Ill., the living room window-wall is curved and placed at brow of the hill to give a wide scan of the lake view. Architects: George Fred and William Keck.

xi.

Owners and architect favored modern. The developer that controls this section in Kansas City, Mo., didn't. He wanted to retain a consistent design flavor in the neighborhood. The result: an effective compromise. Conservative exterior retains simplicity, yet can blend with traditional; interior is as the owners, the Cumonows, like it. Architects: Kivett & Myers.

xii.

CHECKLIST FOR PLANNING INTERIORS

The idea of "building now, decorating later," is not only old fashioned, but downright extravagant. Structure and interior design are inseparable. A master plan for furnishings should be drawn up right along with the blueprints, and their cost figured in the total budget for the house. This program applies whether you are building in everything that can be nailed down, or planning to use family heirlooms. Consider:

Floor-coverings. Wall-to-wall carpeting can go over an inexpensive, unfinished base. Floors of asphalt, cork, rubber, plastic or clay tile permit the use of island rugs.

Wall treatments. Exterior materials are moving indoors. Stone, wood, painted block or brick need no further "decoration." Wallboard can come prefinished, or ready to receive a coating of paper, plastic, fabric or paint. So with plaster. Ease of surface maintenance, or need for replacement, should enter into your choice.

Window treatments. Distinctly a function of architectural design and sun control. Perhaps a built-in track to hold heavy draperies. Perhaps no draperies at all, but venetian blinds, or reeded roll shades, or louvered shutters.

Lighting. This goes beyond enough well-placed outlets. Intensity of light should range from low for mood or indolence to bright for exacting visual tasks. It doesn't cost any more to have the right light in the right place.

Furnishings. Storage pieces are disappearing into the walls, which now hold china, shirts, radios as well as the familiar books. Counter space can be built in, or be provided by a traditional piece. Don't be misled that finished carpentry with the quality of furniture is inexpensive, or that good workmen are easy to find. A handicraft talent helps here. But the fewer the separate pieces of bulky furniture, the larger a small room seems.

The newest standing pieces have been slimmed down so they do not block a view through a window wall, or clutter a room. New frame

Closet, dresser drawers and desk in boy's room are all built in. Gerson Hirsch house, Pleasantville, N.Y. Many new furniture pieces have a sleek built-in look.

materials and foam rubber give comfort and strength without excess padding.

Couches that double as guest beds can slide into wall niches to achieve proper seat depth. Some couches and chairs yield economical extra sleep-space by ingenious unfolding. Major couches to divide large living areas must be "good four sides" and are a vital element in planning and investment. Save money for them.

Colors and fabrics. In a room that partakes of the out-of-doors, it is well to choose a scheme that blends with the natural soft greys, browns, greens, autumn oranges. Add bright accents in small doses. Rough-textured fabrics reflect the trend toward use of natural materials indoors.

Again, interiors should express the people who live in them, and replaceable parts should be considered as a field for whim. The simpler the backgrounds, the more the opportunity for self-expression that marks a house as yours.

Houses for One

There are several delightful things about a house designed for one. Privacy is total. Green can be chartreuse, or pink, shocking. There is no need for compromise—on dreams.

But a wary thought. In spite of the best plans for the rest of a lifetime, many things can happen. Surprising and good things. A new job or partner may mean a change of scene. A house, that cannot be resold to at least a couple is not a good investment.

This need not counter individual plans, because built into the best single houses is the opportunity to entertain family or friends. The over-night guest department is expressed with a little more separation than in a family house —for the benefit of you, the visitors, and if you care, the neighbors.

2 Six reinforced concrete piers make this aerial perch secure. Cost of unusual foundation was balanced by economy of lot. (No. 1 on plan)

(No. 2) Face of house from road is deceptively unassuming. Garage at left forms bridge to living section.

A PROFESSOR PREFERS A HILLTOP HOUSE

Location . . . . SEATTLE, WASHINGTON
Architects . . . JAMES CHIARELLI, PAUL KIRK
Owner . . . . PROF. GEORGE A. LUNDBERG

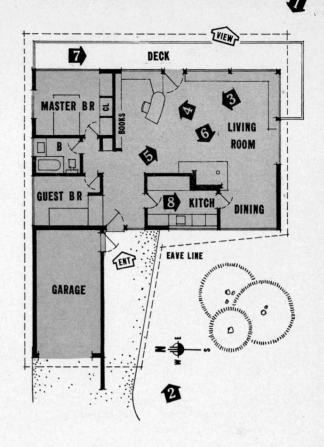

The needs of Professor Lundberg, a bachelor and head of the Sociology Department at the University of Washington, were simple but well-defined. He wanted a view, privacy and a stimulating setting for creative study . . . a place to entertain, but no great menage to care for. Price was to be moderate.

The result: a site in a neighborhood usually expensive because of the spectacular view, but bargain-priced to the professor since hill was considered too steep to build on. Architect solved the lot and living needs with a neat plan and ingenious structure.

Seminars with students around the fire add good living to deep thinking. Professor's study corner in rear. Built-in cabinets in foreground give extra storage for research material, provide overflow seating space. (No. 3 on plan)

Custom desk in an arc, counter space over files, and bookshelves keep thinking material within a 360° reach—served by a swivel chair. Door at right leads to terrace. Shape of desk allows easy traffic. (No. 4 on plan)

Kitchen shares brick wall with fireplace, has window of opaque glass for privacy. (8)

Plan permits help-yourself entertaining—easy on the host for student gatherings. But dining room is formal enough for a Dean. (6)

View sweeps Lake Washington and Mt. Rainier. Height gives sense of isolation from surrounding city. . . . is practical for sun-bathing, too. (5)

Draw draperies across the view windows permit a cloistered feeling for more thoughtful moments . . . also shut out Eastern morning sun. (5)

Downlights illumine deck that hangs in space and darkness, as peaceful as a ship. (7)

5

END

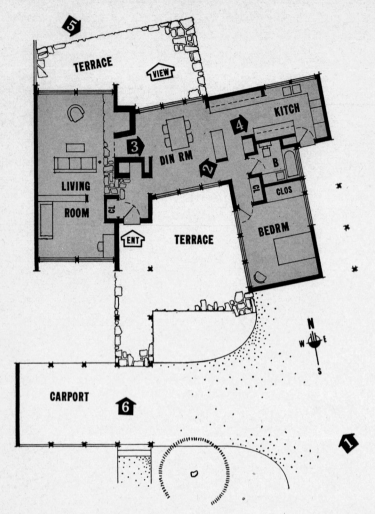

TERRACE
VIEW
KITCH
DIN RM
LIVING ROOM
B
CL
CLOS
ENT
TERRACE
BEDRM
CARPORT

Location . . . . **LAKE STEVENS, near EVERETT, WASHINGTON**
Architects . . . **BASSETTI & MORSE**
Owner . . . . . **MRS. G. J. ARMBRUSTER**

The irregular, open plan is designed to capture as much of the out-of-doors and sun as possible in a northern climate. In the summer, the terrace on the north and lake side is favored. For chillier seasons, the wind-sheltered south terrace (1), below. The center clerestory windows assure light to the innermost areas, no matter what the month. Service entrance at right.

6

IN A YEAR-ROUND VACATION HOUSE ON A LAKE

Above (2), sliding glass walls open up dining room to terrace on fine days. Eye-level fireplace counteracts the bad ones. Serving is easy for one or many from adjacent kitchen, below. (3)

Though this could be a delightful resort house for anyone, it is home for a widow whose grown children are frequent week-end visitors. A curtain draws in the living room to make a sleeping alcove. Even with luxury touches, the cost of the house was modest.

The decoration is part of the scheme to relate the indoors and outdoors. Flagstones in brown, blue and gray tones pave both terraces, as well as the living and dining room floors. Pumice blocks are used for double fireplace wall and exterior masonry.

This house won a first prize for architectural excellence in the Washington State A.I.A. judging, 1951.

(4) Pullman-type kitchen leads into laundry at far end, rounds corner to service entry.

(5) North terrace. Kitchen, dining room and living room all share a view of the lake.

(6) Covered walk links outlying carport to house and entrance, through south terrace. Bedroom at right gets the benefit of Western sun—and sunsets.

END

A DOCTOR ENJOYS THE OUT-OF-DOORS ONLY FIVE MILES FROM WORK

Location . . . . HARWINTON, CONN.
Architect . . . . JOSEPH STEIN
Owner . . . . . DR. S. G. WEISS

Dr. Weiss has an enviable way of life. A bachelor eye specialist, he is just a few minutes' drive from a year-round sportsman's retreat. A garage-barn (not shown) houses two riding horses. A lake for fishing and swimming is only yards away. There is winter skiing.

The doctor started out preferring old Colonial houses, evolved this unusual structure. Above (1), roof slope is steep to shed snow. The balcony leads off top-story bedroom.

(2) Air-borne stairway is made of oak treads solidly bolted into stone wall. It leads to balcony bedroom of generous size. Behind balcony face are cabinets, open shelves, bed-light and head-board.

10

Plan is essentially one large room with two-deck arrangement of bedroom over kitchen, all fitting neatly under the high point of the roof. Bath on ground floor is practical for general use—and causes no problem of privacy in a house for one. Plans allow for expansion, if and when desired.

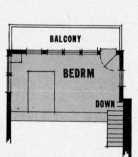

(3) Skier-owner at main entrance. Angled chimney adds structural interest to small house, inside and out.

(4) Effective setting for a bachelor. Fireplace is designed for extra heat, windows admit southern sun.

END

A ONE-ROOM DESIGN SOLVES A BUDGET HOUSING PROBLEM

Location . . . . **FAYETTEVILLE, ARKANSAS**
Architect . . . . **PROF. MICHAEL STOUSLAND**
Owners . . . . **THE MICHAEL STOUSLANDS**

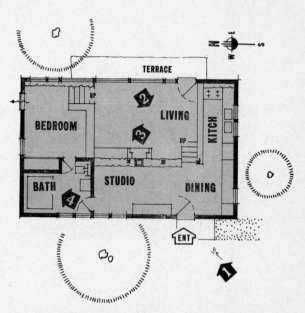

(2) Stairs lead from living room to kitchen, dining area and entrance on balcony level.

(1) The balcony level becomes a ground floor, as the house meets the slope of the hill.

(3) Openable windows at bottom permit an unobstructed view down the hill. Corner stairway leads to bedroom.

Professor Stousland, in the Architecture Department at the University of Arkansas had just as much trouble finding a place to live as anyone else on a campus.

He and his wife took matters into their own hands and built a house for only $7,000. It is really one large room, partitioned by a U-shaped balcony 3 ft. above the main level. The device gives spaciousness in a tiny structure that measures only 24 ft. by 36 ft. A couple lives here, but the design is especially good for a single person.

(4) The sunken tub is a favorite place for neighbors' children to play on a hot day. Fish mobiles help the fun.

END

A TRAVELED LADY SETTLES DOWN—AND CHOOSES MODERN THAT IS EASY TO KEEP NEAT

A long, interesting life gives this owner more reason than most to have a house bulging with a collection of mementos. Yet the lady, generously above sixty, edited her possessions to a favorite few, and uses them as accents in a house almost starkly simple—to her choice.

Her taste meant that she could realize a house far lower in cost than its convenience suggests, and one that takes little work.

Location . . . . **ANDOVER, MASSACHUSETTS**
Architects . . . **THE ARCHITECTS COLLABORATIVE**
Owner . . . . . **AN ELDERLY SINGLE LADY**

(1) The open plan of the living room with its free-standing fireplace gives extra space to a small room.

(2) The entrance says welcome, and sunshine streams in through the glass wall, even though windows are omitted on this side for privacy. The single horizontal window is in the kitchen.

(3) Touches from South American travel are used succinctly to decorate the straightforward structure. The redwood wall runs cleanly through the house, indoors and out.

(5) The owner's neatness is revealed in the kitchen, too. Stove and sink are scaled to her needs, as well as cabinets. There is no requirement for sudden expansion of entertainment facilities, so hospitality is tailored to receive a few good friends. The window over the sink looks out to the entrance road.

(6) The bedroom wing, with redwood wall, is formed of concrete block. Its solidity is tempered with the poise of the cantilevered living room.

(4) Bedroom window frames a look to the woods. All window and door trim, all built-in cabinets and hardware are kept as simple as possible—a taste that is gentle on the budget and easy to care for.

END

Good Small Houses

A "little house" has many meanings. It can be for two who have just married and plan for children, or for those who are having them currently. It can be for a couple who have seen their children marry and leave, and want to pare down their living to size. It can be for people who never built a house before, or never cared, but suddenly there is something about a garden or a dog.

Whatever it is, it is a beginning. There is no single answer in design to these varied desires—except to be small in area and inexpensive. The best formula is to plan well and make the rooms flexible, for many uses. Some of these good small houses that answer special requirements do as well for others. Think of them that way.

CONTEMPORARY WITH A COUNTRY AIR

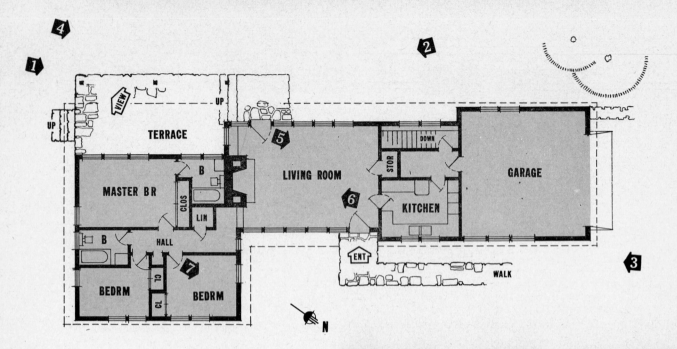

Location .... **CORNWALL BRIDGE, CONN.**
Architect .... **WILLIAM LESCAZE**
Owners ..... **THE SYDNEY M. KAYES**

This is the story of a mature couple who live in a New York city apartment. Both are busy in town, but have thought ahead to build a summer house that will eventually become a year-round permanent home. The Kayes wanted a living atmosphere that harmonized with the natural setting, and one quite distinct from the sophistication of their city apartment.

The use of redwood siding and local stone carry out the flavor of a house in the woods. The plan and location preserve the best of the site, and give the Kayes one more thing they desired—convenience for living and entertaining without a maid. Though designed for a couple, this house could handle two with children.

(3) Above. Garden beside entry walk makes a pretty and practical transition from the parking area.

(2) Left. Door from living room leads onto step-down terrace with a long view.

(1) Right. Man and nature collaborated on decorative pool—which is also fine for swimming.

Mrs. Kaye had great fun with this house, for she pursued her own enthusiasms about collecting Colonial antiques. The simple forms by early American furniture craftsmen blend easily with modern architecture in the woods. She chose tawny tones —beiges, wood browns, and tangerine accents—to balance the wealth of outdoor green.

(5) Above, left. Pine sideboard and dining chairs date from the late 1700's, were found on a scouting trip in Vermont.

(7) Old pine dressing chest is authentic. Small-patterned contemporary chintz reflects Colonial flavor, is echoed in valances.

(4) Strategic location—at the crest of a rise and backed by trees—gives this small house importance.

(6) Stone from the property was used for fireplace. The coffee table is a pine seat from an old sleigh.

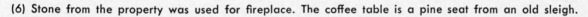

END

(1) A short driveway-that-becomes-carport handles automobile needs inexpensively. The overhang shields the walk to main entrance. Door to the kitchen is handy.

(4) Folding doors, closed at left, present a handsome face to the living room, and conceal work-in-progress or children at play. Below, open, they reveal extra space for entertaining, really make one large room out of the two.

24

FLEXIBILITY
IS THE SECRET
OF THIS SMALL HOUSE

Location .... SEATTLE, WASHINGTON
Architect.... PAUL HAYDEN KIRK
Owners .... THE GEORGE TAVERNITES

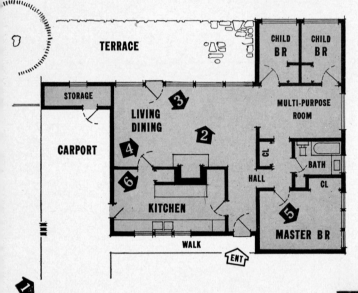

(3) A fire feels good for at least three seasons in Seattle. This amenable feature was possible in a modest house, by keeping fireplace design very simple.

The Tavernites are a young couple who figured their future into their house, so that it can change as they do. The key to this adaptability is the "multi-purpose" room, which started as a music room for the composer-pianist wife. Just recently, when small son Mark became five, he and the television set moved in and took over. Should there be another child, it will have a bedroom and playroom all ready.

A lot of living convenience has been designed into this house, which cost only $10,000.

25

(2) The small living room seems larger with walls of glass on the garden side. The door at left provides easy access to the terrace.

(5) Transom panels above fixed windowpanes open for ventilation in bedroom.

(6) Knotty pine gives kitchen a rural character. Laundry department is at far end.

END

CAPE COD HOUSE
REFLECTS
ITS HERITAGE

Location . . . . COHASSET, MASS.
Architect . . . . ROYAL BARRY WILLS
Owners . . . . THE R. B. WILLS

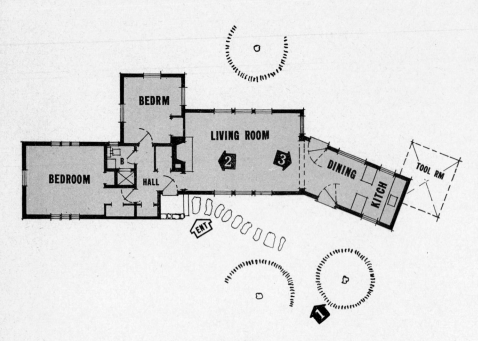

A capsule of New England sentiment-by-the-sea, this summer house could be lived in the year round. Mrs. Wills would not mind, as she loves the water, and the contemporary plan is angled to give a view of it from every room.

The house is tiny, but quite ample to handle visiting children and grandchildren, who practically live in their swimming suits. Outdoor meals, on the sea-side terrace just off the dining room, are sparked with a spectacular view. Sheltered south terrace allows outdoor dining late into the fall.

(1) Walk leads to vine-covered entrance. Griffin holding lantern guards Dutch-door entrance to dining room. Over-scaled chimney is a trademark of architect Wills. It makes a house look smaller and cozier.

28

Part of the nostalgic charm—and economy—of this house comes from the reclaimed materials. (3) Above, old ship's knees frame dining space, window shutters make pass-door to the kitchen.

(2) Old panel doors form fireplace wall. Bargain windows from a barn have been chewed by a horse.

END

(1) Side facing the street has a minimum of window area. Stepped-back entrance lends interest to simple plan.

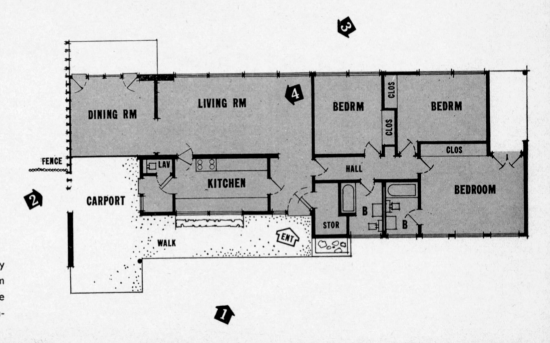

(3) Garden side gives full play to windows, since no problem of privacy is involved. The overhang modifies the southern sun. (Below)

ECONOMICAL HOUSE: RESULT OF GOOD PLANNING

Location . . . . SHREVEPORT, LOUISIANA
Architect . . . . WILLIAM B. WIENER
Owners . . . . THE ELMER SIMONS

By a canny use of materials, and a plan that acknowledges cost limitations, a good architect can make the best of a budget.

William Wiener did just that for the Simons. The rectangular plan with its simple roof and foundations kept the building bids down. So did the frank use of exterior materials inside—such as the painted brick in the living room.

The Simons wanted a separate dining room, but rather than a wall which would have made both rooms seem smaller, a visual break was established with china cabinets and a cross-beam. The cabinet backs supply extra wall space to the living room, too.

A house need not be dull, just because it is built economically. Proof is below, right, where studs are used in an ingenious way for decoration. The sapling fence not only adds its handsome touch, but confines the children's play-yard and provides family privacy.

(4) One room looks like two with the device of a semi-partition.

(2) Studs are placed on the outside, sheathing on the inside, to make an interesting exterior pattern at low cost.

END

HOT CLIMATE HOUSE TRAPS BREEZES

Location .... **FRESNO, CALIFORNIA**
Architects ... **WURSTER, BERNARDI & EMMONS**
Owners .... **THE M. P. DAVISONS**

The evolution of the Davison house has a moral in it for those who think that a lot of house is necessary. It was built as a guest house, the first unit of a larger scheme. The Davisons found the simple living so gratifying, they abandoned previous plans, and added an even smaller structure to lodge their teen-age sons. With riding and swimming and gardening, there is recreation for everyone.

(2) The swimming pool is just two steps away from the front porch. Adjacent guest and bathing house was designed by Paul Oppenheim to reflect the spirit of the main house.

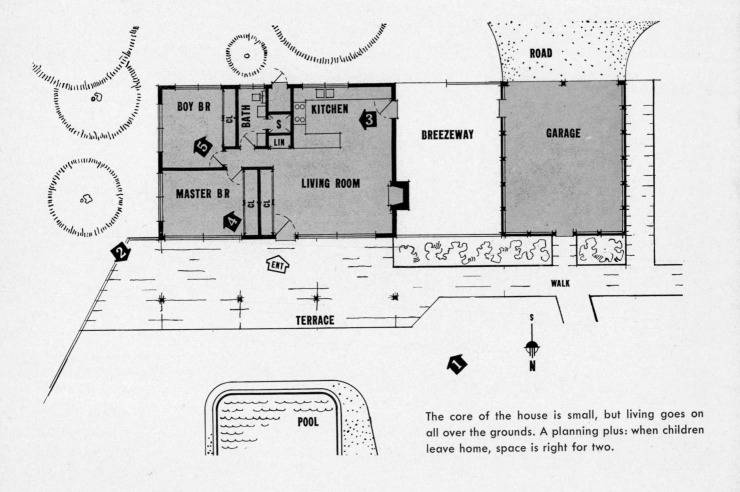

32

The core of the house is small, but living goes on all over the grounds. A planning plus: when children leave home, space is right for two.

(1) The front porch is a hard-working part of the living area, with comfortable chairs and a table for outdoor dining. The batten-board exterior is typically Western. Garage is at extreme right, with drying yard behind fence.

33

(3) The unusual roof line, left, and above, has a purpose in a hot California valley—sometimes breathlessly hot. The break catches whatever random breeze, and funnels it through the house for cooling. The height carries off the hot air, too. Vent fan over stove keeps cooking odors from mixing with general air circulation. Dining space at left.

CONTINUED, HOT CLIMATE HOUSE

(5) Boy's or guest bedroom has one bed that slides out of way into corner headboard. This space-saving trick is easy to build at home. Note runners at bottom.

(4) Heavy family furniture is in scale with the high ceiling, and contributes sentiment to the master bedroom. Louvers at top define the break in the roof, give good ventilation. The sliding door opens directly onto the front terrace.

END

TINY, TRIM MODERN HOUSE USES SPACE WELL

Location .... **YELLOW SPRINGS, OHIO**
Architect .... **MAX G. MERCER**
Owners .... **A YOUNG COUPLE**

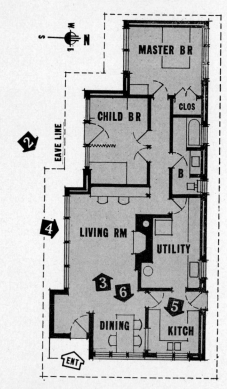

This house was designed for a young couple with two pre-school age children. They wanted the small ones to have free wheeling between the outdoor play area and their bedroom and bath, but not through the living room. Above (2) shows the door from the children's room to the bricked terrace. This side of the house is opened to the south to catch the winter sun. Note on the plan that privacy for each child —or communal play—is an ad lib choice in their bedroom, with a sliding curtain and separate interior doors.

(1) Main entrance is at narrow end. Twin house is across the street.

35

(2) The decorative horizontal lines on the exterior towards the terrace are open louvers for ventilation under fixed glass panes. Below, note how the plywood panel "opens the window." Screens are built in permanently. Brick, set in earth at right angles, makes an attractive, economical terrace.

(3) Both parents wanted desk space, but the budget would not allow an extra room for a study. They answered this with built-in twin desks, easy to build, or assemble from stock cabinets. The long, single counter does for two, or yields extra elbow room when one has work to spread out.

36

(5) and (6), right. Pass-counter from kitchen to dining room permits conversation and easy serving or clean-up. Shelves with pretty china block a too-clear view. Dining table is in a jog off the living room.

(4) Recessed fireplace does not intrude on a narrow room. Simple face decorated only with masks helps this feeling, as well as the lack of hearth.

END

A HOUSE WITH EASY ENTERTAINMENT BUILT IN

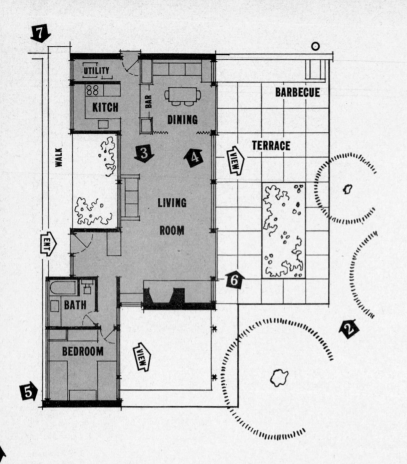

Location . . . . **RALEIGH, NORTH CAROLINA**
Architect . . . . **PROF. GEORGE MATSUMOTO**
Owners . . . . **THE J. G. POOLES**

This is truly a house for a party—quiet or gay, for two or many, in winter or summer. Though designed for week-end fun, it could be a permanent home for two who enjoy friends.

The house divides cleanly into bedroom privacy for the owners—and the rest of the house to the guests. A skillful planning of furniture and built-ins packs a lot of service into a really small house. Note (on plan) the cabinet at the entrance. Its break creates a foyer; it is a coat closet on the hall side and a radio-phonograph-game department facing the living room.

(1) Below. A well-conceived house becomes its setting.

(2) The terrace and window walls make the most of the lake view. Large end panes are really sliding doors, opening up both the living and dining rooms to the out-of-doors.

(7) Modest entry holds a surprise—a plant bed midway.

(5) Owner's bedroom is tiny but ample. Window through which photograph was taken matches the one shown. Thus, good moving air is assured—important in the South.

(3) Below, asymmetric pattern of brick and stone gives interest to the firelace, and makes it a focal point at the end of a long room. Vine and tray rest on jutting stones. Desk niche balances wood storage corner at left.

40

(4) This room is full of double-use tricks, essential in a small house. Above, it is an admirable cocktail lounge. The kitchen is just over the counter to the left. Comes dining time, curtains pull to conceal preparations from the living room, legs flip up on the low coffee table, and it is the right height for serving, as shown left. . . . There's more. The wall couch, with bedding beneath, rolls out. A blind drops over the counter. And the room quarters over-night guests. The ingenuity in furnishings is part of the planning by the architect, a professor at North Carolina State College.

(6) Good dining goes on outdoors, too, with a barbecue fireplace. This terminates a long counter for serving or seating. Center table is an old millstone on blocks.

END

Planned for Children and Adults

The more the merrier is a fine saying, but it can work in reverse unless thought is taken to respect the rights of large and small individuals. The right to romp belongs to everyone. Also the right to privacy. The house that provides for both generations is a good family house.

Specifications: A chance for parents and children to enjoy each other. A chance for man and wife to be alone together, which is why they married in the first place. A chance for children to imagine freely in their own wonderful world. A chance for grown-up guests to feel at ease, even if they don't like children.

Secret of a house that becomes all things to all people is a wise plan, permitting division of activities. Let young and adult share or separate. In extreme cases, acoustic materials are helpful!

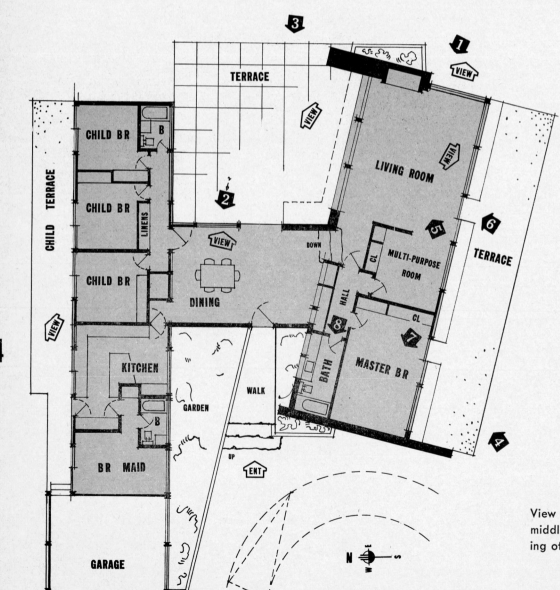

3

TERRACE

1

VIEW

VIEW

CHILD BR

B

VIEW

LIVING ROOM

VIEW

CHILD TERRACE

CHILD BR

LINENS

VIEW

DOWN

5

6

CL

MULTI-PURPOSE

ROOM

TERRACE

CHILD BR

DINING

2

44

VIEW

CL

HALL

8

7

KITCHEN

GARDEN

WALK

BATH

MASTER BR

B

BR MAID

UP

ENT

N E W S

GARAGE

View above (1 on plan), shows the middle and adult terraces and the feeling of closeness to the desert.

THIS IS A FAMILY— AND A HOUSE FOR BIG AND SMALL

Location . . . . PHOENIX, ARIZONA
Architect. . . . EDWARD VARNEY
Owners . . . . THE EDWARD VARNEYS

The Varney solution for two-generation enjoyment is forthright and full of human understanding. The plan tells the story best. It is really a house with three terraces—one for adults, one for children, and one to be shared. To each his own.

On the children's side, maid or mother can keep a watchful eye, even in the kitchen. This play yard is well away from vehicles. The adult terrace on the south side receives cool breezes in the evening, when parents want to relax—or hide. The sheltered center terrace is best for winter.

Indoors, big and small can play their own games separately, with the wing arrangement of the house. The connecting link is the dining room-hall-foyer.

Despite the out-of-the-way looks of the site, it is really 2½ acres of native desert, located in a suburb. The city can be seen to the south, and spectacular mountains to the north and east. In fact, the living room was angled purposely to capture three views.

One other factor decided the orientation— the hot Arizona sun. With all the window walls, this could be a menace rather than a delight. The house is so located that no direct sunlight reaches any glass area after 8:30 a.m. during the summer months. The roof overhangs are calculated to control the sun's intrusion. A cooling system compensates, too.

45

The Family: Father. Mother, with Squaw Peak in the background. Two children watching television with two visiting friends. Two more Varneys in the nursery. Total score: girl, ten; boys: seven, three, and one.

(2) Hospitality is relaxed and genuine at the Varneys, but there is planning back of its smoothness. In contrast to houses where the living room, dining room and kitchen flow into one another, here the three rooms are kept separate. Meals, junior-grade, and bedtime proceed unobtrusively during adult fun. A later move to the living room takes the party even farther away from assorted early sleepers.

(3) The middle terrace leads directly off the dining room, and is often used for outdoor meals. Garden beds rim the patio and soften surroundings. Non-desert plants thrive because of the partial shade—and hand-watering.

(4) Though terrace faces south, the roof overhang and terminal wall of stone keep a too-hot sun from heating glass. Living room and bedroom open directly on this adult retreat.

(5) The slight step-down of the living room gives a sheltered feeling, even though the room is open visually on three sides. A Chinese rug adds soft color and pattern to otherwise simple, light-toned decoration. Sheer curtains modify sunlight.

47

(7) Master bedroom shares common stone wall with bathroom, opposite. Over-sized double bed is built against wall of random-width brown ash. Ceilings throughout the house are V-jointed hemlock, painted grey-green.

48

(6) Living room windows frame mountain view. Steel beams are sheathed in copper, which will be allowed to take on its natural multi-colored patina.

49

Contrasting textures distinguish this dressing-bath. Native stone and walnut plywood are played against smooth glass, chrome and ceramic tile. (8)

END

A ticklish problem—to blend a modern house with the most traditional of localities. This was accomplished by crafty exterior and interior design. Above (3), dining is pleasant with heritage chairs and a whopping view window. Bookcases reach to the ceiling. Right (4), the corner eye-level fireplace is as old as it is new. The rocker has a history; the print above is frankly modern. Both eras are united in the contemporary primitive pattern of the bedspread.

(2) The Hays cannot share the Varney freedom with terraces (page 44) because of weather. Trees are twisted by the northeastern blows. So the L-shaped house has its back to the wind, and shelters a sunning spot.

WORKS PRIVATELY AT HOME

Location . . . . BREWSTER, MASSACHUSETTS

Architect . . . . ROBERT WOODS KENNEDY

Owners . . . . THE JOHN HAYS

Mr. Hay has a special reason for privacy. He works at home. Not only is his study located at the far end of the house, away from noisy family activity, but it is separated acoustically by a fireplace and two doors.

Noise goes two ways. The Hays particularly enjoy musical parties, with dancing and ad lib painting or whatever. The children (two) can sleep peacefully through it all. On the plans note cut-off for bedroom wing, as well as easy kitchen arrangement for guests.

(1) The elbow end of the house shows the bedroom wing to the right, and the entry porch to the left, which makes for very fine sitting, come sundown.

51

END

(1) Living room and bedrooms open onto terrace with wading pool. Lanscaping by architect.

52

(2) Bedroom for 3-year-old girl adjoins outdoor play space. Chest stows both toys and clothes.

A HOUSE THAT LOOKS LARGER THAN IT IS

The Semples and their architect played tricks with looks. An unusual entrance—a portico of open-work brick, favorite material in this area—leads into a low-ceilinged hall. This approach gives unexpected drama to the first glimpse of the living room, which has natural ceiling height. Window walls at the far end carry the eye out for an even longer look.

On the private side, porch, overhang and terrace expand the living area beyond the true house. And all on a budget.

Location . . . . **LADUE, ST. LOUIS COUNTY, MISSOURI**
Architect . . . . **HARRIS ARMSTRONG**
Owners . . . . **THE FREDERICK SEMPLES**

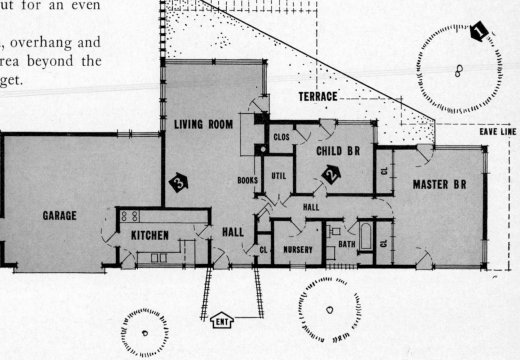

Right, the plan shows the long view through the house from entrance to terrace. Nursery is for a brand-new child, testimony to planning foresight in including an "overflow" room, even for a budget house.

(3) To have or have not a mantel often starts a lively debate between architect and owner. Most modern designs call for a smooth face above a fireplace opening—to avoid a feeling of clutter. But some people, particularly in the Midwest, need a mantel to feel at home. This one is low and simple, and integrated with the bookshelves and radio-TV center. Living room overlooks gardens.

53

END

FOR BUSY PARENTS AND FOUR OLDER CHILDREN

Location . . . . **HOUSTON, TEXAS**
Architect . . . . **HAMILTON BROWN**
Owners . . . . **THE JUDGE WILMER B. HUNTS**

The sleek floor opposite belongs to several people: two teen-age daughters who like to dance; two sons who prefer sliding at the moment; and a mother who paints. The lily pool is really a moat to keep her easels inviolate from rampant youth.

Again, the plan tells the story of the house best. There are two rooms for the girls with a bath between, and extra dressing space. The boys have the same in a more manly fashion. Each bedroom has its own sunning terrace.

Judge Hunt, who likes his privacy, can retreat to the master bedroom, well-removed from the active household. Sliding doors open onto a separate terrace, calculated for parental seclusion.

(4) In this open plan, the rug defines a smaller area for cozy moments around the fire. Same spot cleared for dancing, right.

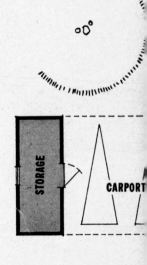

STORAGE

CARPORT

(1) Boys' terrace, off their bedrooms, is on entrance side of house. Girls' terrace is private.

(2) The Big Room is purposely designed wide open to handle high jinks for any number. It is a favorite gathering spot for other teen-agers—the family idea behind it.

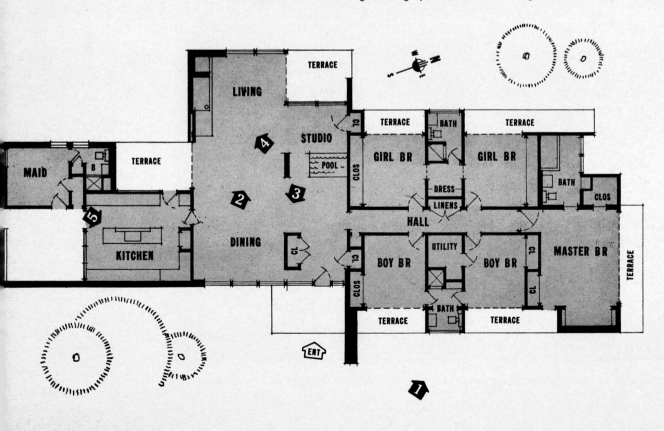

(3) The free-standing pier serves as a coat closet and a break between entrance and dining room area. Serving pass-door to kitchen is at extreme right.

56

(5) Island counter protects cook from the boys, who use the hall as a raceway to play yard. Pass-door to dining room appears in reveal to the rear.

END

COMPACT TWO-STORY DESIGN SERVES SEVEN CHILDREN

Location . . . . SOUTH BEND, INDIANA
Architect . . . . WILLIAM LESCAZE
Owners . . . . THE JEROME CROWLEYS

The Crowleys lead a happy, if complicated, life with a stair-step family—four boys and three girls ranging from twelve to one year old. The top floor now is essentially a barracks, and is operated as such. A playroom is in the basement.

The problem here was to avoid building a too-big house, that would be unpleasantly empty as successive children went off to school. The two-story plan, below (1), gives the most space, and blends into a Midwestern suburb, even though modern in character.

Mr. Crowley is the president of The O'Brien Corporation, a paint company. Naturally, with seventy fingerprints to be wiped off daily, he chose his product for inside and outside surfaces.

57

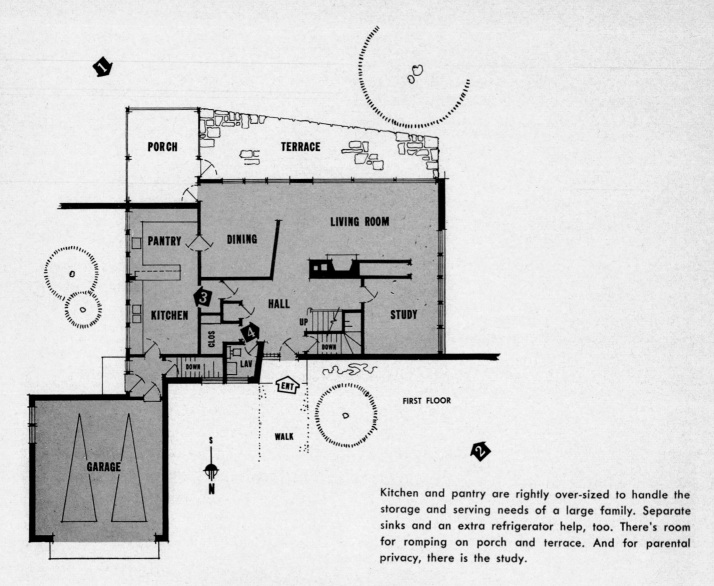

PORCH

TERRACE

LIVING ROOM

PANTRY

DINING

KITCHEN

HALL

STUDY

CLOS

LAV

DOWN

UP

DOWN

ENT

WALK

GARAGE

FIRST FLOOR

Kitchen and pantry are rightly over-sized to handle the storage and serving needs of a large family. Separate sinks and an extra refrigerator help, too. There's room for romping on porch and terrace. And for parental privacy, there is the study.

58

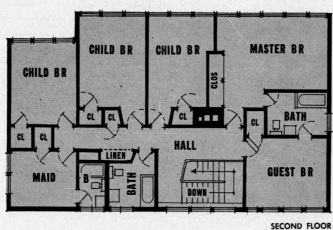

CHILD BR

CHILD BR

CHILD BR

MASTER BR

CLOS

CL

CL

CL

CL

BATH

CL

CL

CL

MAID

B

LINEN

BATH

HALL

GUEST BR

DOWN

SECOND FLOOR

With population at its current peak, guests must double up as well as the young ones. But if the guests didn't like children, they wouldn't be visiting!

(2) Only a minimum of windows face the street. The butterfly roof is designed to lighten the looks of the top floor.

(3) Counter break in kitchen helps segregate customers from cooks. Assembly-line lunches are available here.

(4) Architectural details are simple and clean, as a background for the preferred traditional furnishings.

END

EAVE LINE

BEDRM | BEDRM | BEDROOM

LIVING

UTILITY | DARKROOM

③

HALL

DINING

CLOS ②

STUDIO

BEDRM | BATH | KITCHEN

ENT

S / N

COURT

EAVE LINE

CARPORT

STORAGE

①

60

Cost was kept down by a compact plan, structural simplicity and the use of local materials—cedar siding and brick, inside and out. Living room opens onto its own terrace.

(2) Studio and darkroom occupy one wing, well removed from body of house and inquisitive young ones. Windows get north light.

STUDIO ARE COMBINED FOR A DENVER PHOTOGRAPHER

Location . . . . **ENGLEWOOD, COLORADO**
near **DENVER**

Architect . . . . **VICTOR HORNBEIN**

Owners . . . . **THE MARSHALL BROOKSES**

This man wraps his living and work in a package, as pictured above (1). The windows of his studio are silhouetted unconventionally against a winter sky; his three children play in the snow.

The Brookses are unconventional people. Mrs. B. is a dancer, and is sharing her talent with the children. Mr. B. can tell a story, or catch a fish, or make a photograph, or enjoy classical music. The house is built to encourage these varied interests or handle any new ones.

(3) Dining room opens onto private court, used for summer meals and served through kitchen window. Furniture was brought from New England.

END

(1) Natural stone above ground lies below as well. A house built on rock is comfor
ing, but its design bows to land levels. Carport is practically located where drive end

(2) Center room is setting for creative play, or just plain horse-play, between parents an
children. Kitchen is adjacent so Mother shares the fun. Bedroom corridor is at right.

YOUNG AND ADULT

Location . . . .
OLD GREENWICH, CONNECTICUT

Architect . . . .
WALTER PROKOSCH

Owners . . . .
The **WALTER PROKOSCHES**

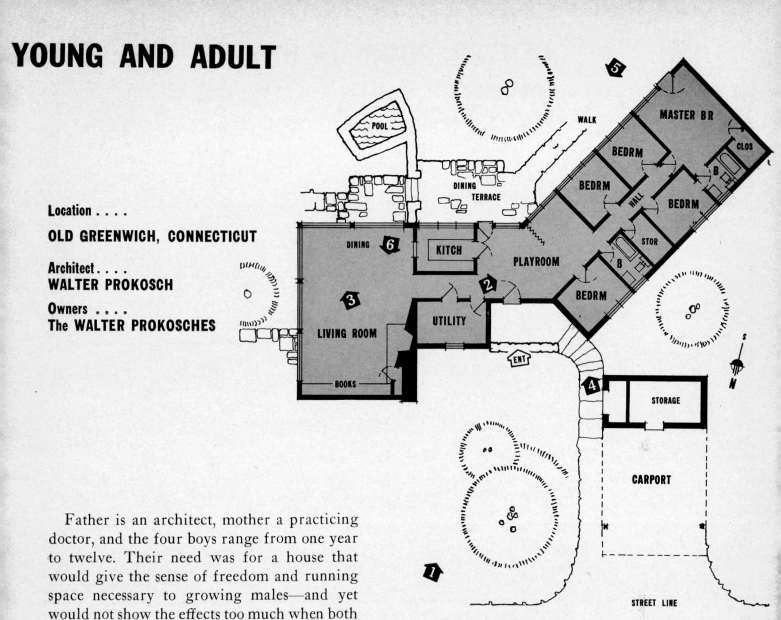

Father is an architect, mother a practicing doctor, and the four boys range from one year to twelve. Their need was for a house that would give the sense of freedom and running space necessary to growing males—and yet would not show the effects too much when both parents returned from work. A nurse looks after the children during the day.

Each child has his own bedroom. All are adjacent to a large center playroom in which anything can happen, and no one cares. This room is also used for family dining, and can be eyed unobtrusively from the kitchen.

The location of the house is a rocky New England site, where leveling with blasting proved impractical. So the house was adjusted to the way the land lies. The main portion with bedrooms and kitchen fits easily on one level, which includes the family terrace. The living room is raised, for reasons of land contours, but this nicely sets off a division of the house not for children.

(3) Dining for adults includes a glimpse of the lily pond, service through kitchen pass-door.

(4) Custom-paneled Dutch doors make a focal point for a dramatic entrance. Redwood siding over concrete block, brick, and stone from site amplify rustic air.

(5) Lower terrace is for child's play and summertime family meals. Up three steps is the lily pool and terrace for adult cavorting.

(6) Living room reflects musical hobby—with double built-in speakers.

END

PLAYROOM IS PRIVATE – BUT EASILY WATCHED

Location . . . . SAN MATEO, CALIFORNIA
Architect . . . . FRED LANGHORST
Owners . . . . THE RICHARD KAUFFMANS

Both living needs and sloping land were the challenge behind this plan. The house was resolved with three levels, stepped up gently. Lowest is for the carport and entrance, with maid's room to the rear. The main living level with its terraces is halfway, and the family bedrooms top the rest. This device neatly divides the special activities of child and adult.

During the day, the Kauffmans prefer to keep a watchful eye on their two young children, without seeming to hover. The playroom is strategically located so it can be sighted from kitchen, dining or living rooms. This room has sliding doors, and doubles for over-night guests. Father has his own playroom—for a photographic hobby.

(2) Playroom is fitted with toy cabinets, counter space and outside door. Sliding panels close off dining room.

(3) A casual glance from master bedroom to child's room suffices. Stairway to middle level is at left.

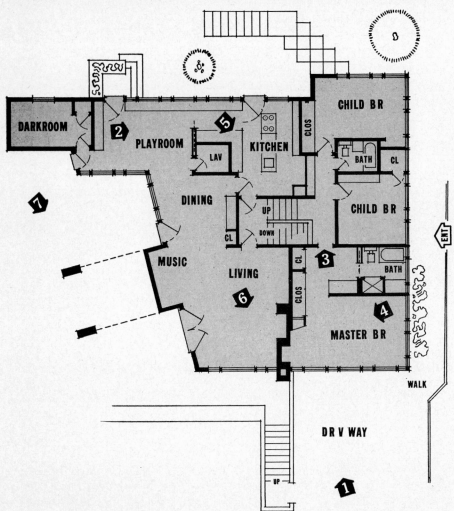

DARKROOM

PLAYROOM

KITCHEN

CHILD BR

CLOS

LAV

BATH

CL

DINING

CHILD BR

UP

CL

DOWN

CL

MUSIC

LIVING

CLOS

BATH

MASTER BR

DR V WAY

UP

WALK

ENT

67

The three levels show above (1), with the bedrooms over the carport. The walk behind the wall leads to the living room terrace. Main and service entrance is at right. Unconventional look is structural solution to difficult land. Note the simple, even roof line, a building economy.

(4) Master bedroom faces front. Street distraction is minimized with small windows. Make-up table gets benefit of daylight, continues counter line when closed. Comforting fireplace shares chimney stack with one below.

(5) Center island containing stove and sink utilizes the best techniques of restaurateurs. Dishwasher and storage is below. Laundry side of kitchen is in foreground, active cooking equipment is easy to reach with open shelves.

(6) Above, fireplace and furnishings fit together. Hearth is also sit-space. Low stone lintel gives the design effect of a mantel, without being one.

(7) Sunning terrace is tied architecturally to the house by brick and wood, which tempers sun with shade. Terrace leads off living room and darkroom.

END

Houses for Limited Lot Lines

No matter what the family requirements, sometimes the starting point for a house is a piece of land. This may be acquired because it is conveniently located, or suddenly available, or inherited, or because of a wild impulse at a tax auction sale.

The city or suburban lot is usually short on frontage, but long on services. Schools and transportation are convenient. City water and disposal is at hand, as well as police and fire protection. Most difficult to achieve is privacy.

The problem is to design a house that fits the land, the family—and provides the extra in outdoor living usually associated with country homes.

A LONG NARROW LOT—
AND A MEMORABLE VIEW

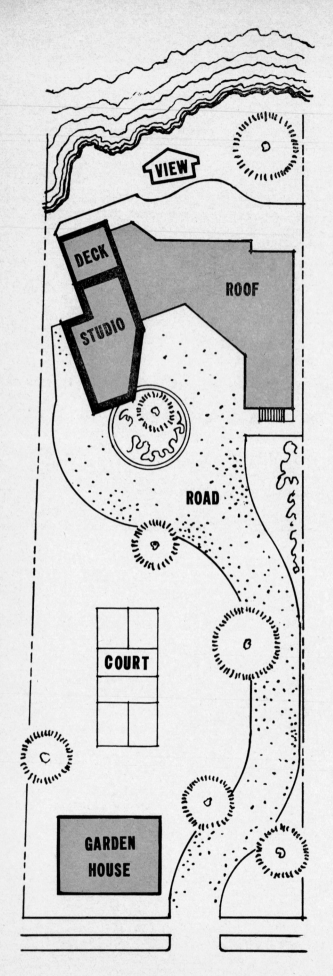

Location .... **SEATTLE, WASHINGTON**
Architect.... **ROGER GOTTELAND**
Owner ..... **THE DR. JOHN LEHMANNS**

The Lehmanns acquired a thin slice from a large estate, terminated with a magnificent view of Puget Sound. Landscaping had a head start of years, so it was desirable to save as many trees and shrubs as possible.

At the same time, the family needs were quite special. Dr. Lehmann is always on call—often at irregular hours. Thus the carport is near the master bedroom, with a separate entrance. Mrs. L. is an exhibiting painter. Her studio is the only second-story room, with sun-deck adjacent. The natural light and isolation necessary for concentration are "perfect," she says.

The children's rooms and working portion of the house are grouped in the right end of the half-moon plan. The convex side of the house misses not one inch of view. Note on plot plan, left, how the curved driveway adds interest and a pleasant element of surprise at its conclusion.

(1) Entrance is in the heart of the turn-around. Photo taken from carport. Roof of second-floor studio shows above.

72

(2) View of the Sound is reflected in window walls.
Stairway at right leads to artist's sundeck.

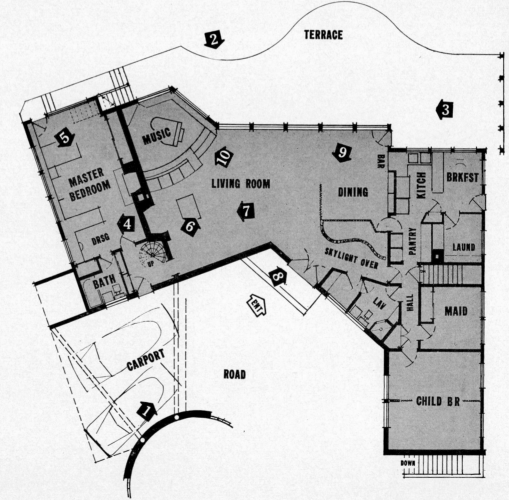

TERRACE

2

3

MUSIC

5

MASTER
BEDROOM

DRSG

4

6

LIVING ROOM

10

7

9

BAR

DINING

KITCH

BRKFST

PANTRY

LAUND

SKYLIGHT OVER

BATH

UP

8

ENT

LAV

HALL

MAID

CARPORT

ROAD

1

CHILD BR

DOWN

73

(10) Right, ingenious step-down of music corner from living room permits an outdoor view over the bulk of grand piano. Record cabinets are below eye level—provide seating for sangerfests. Top break becomes couch-back for fireside groupings. The Lehmanns have a duet—Mrs. on the piano, Mr. on the clarinet, while the children play games in a space big enough to wear them out for bedtime.

(3) Terrace is more than a view-catcher. Informal dining is simple, just off the kitchen. Business can be transacted with an outdoor phone. As much time as possible is spent in this pleasant spot.

(5) Below, bedroom fireplace is used constantly in winter. Far door opens on circular staircase that leads up to studio and down to living room or carport. (4) Left, dressing niche is formed by built-out cupboard and writing desk.

Skylight illumines core of house, entrance (8) and dining room (9). Plants
thrive beneath and decorate service path to kitchen. Other side of common
wall holds serving shelf. Kitchen is behind wall with refreshments.

(6) Whole house focuses on view. Colors tie in with surroundings—grey predominates, green second, hot red on sofa.

(7) The Lehmanns chose to spend for space rather than expensive finishes. Living room measures 50 ft. by 25 ft. Vertical jointing in brickwork provides counterpoint to the horizontal look created by beams and bricks themselves, typical of the Northwest. House won 1952 A.I.A. award for best in Washington State.

77

END

HOUSE WITH TWO FACES IN A SUBURB

Location . . . . EGGERTSVILLE, NEW YORK
near BUFFALO

Architects . . . FOIT & BASCHNAGEL

Owners . . . . THE ALFRED G. BASCHNAGELS

The design problem of the Baschnagels could be repeated in towns and suburbs across the country—a 70 ft. frontage and what to do with it. Here the owners had a plus, with mature foliage shielding them from the road. Thus they were able to create a private front garden and justify a picture window. In the rear is the eating terrace and general play space.

In plan, the house is zoned. Bedrooms can be cut off. The center section handles entertaining inside or out. Winter headquarters for the young son and his friends is the basement recreation room, with access—on wet-boot days—through the garage, and an easy path to the kitchen.

(3) One face—toward the play yard and picnic area. This terrace is easily served from the kitchen.

(4) Left. Front face is a picture window, usually unwise on a street side. But here, the outlook is walled by trees.

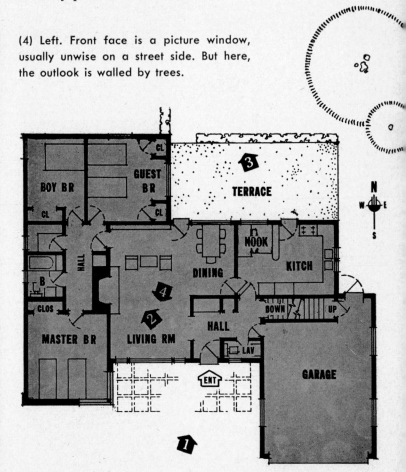

78

(1) Outside of house has sufficient traditional flavor to please a conservative community. Slotted overhang to shield window from sun is modern, is cleverly made part of clean roof line from bedroom section, left, to garage at right.

(2) On winter days, guests pause here. In summer, they walk through to the terrace, through curtained portion. Door to left closes off bedroom section completely. Lavatory serves guests. Cabinets under bookcases hold bridge table and chairs.

END

PARTIAL TWO-STORY PLAN CONSERVES SPACE

(1) Eye-catching height of entrance, accented with columns, gives excitement to house that spurns the street.

(2) Foreground chairs and table separate living and dining ends of long room, close a conversation circle around the fireplace. They can easily be pushed back when the party is a big one.

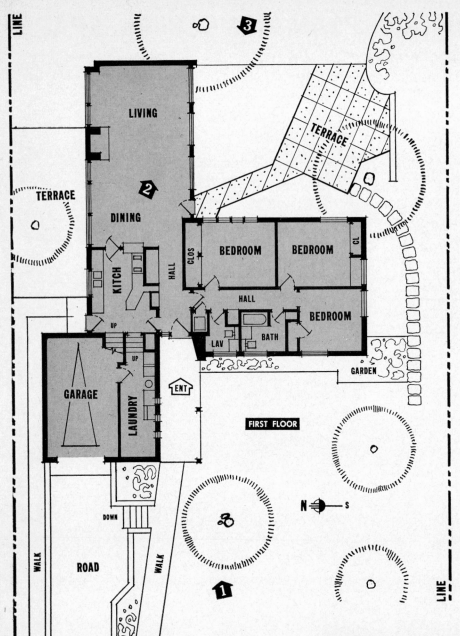

LINE

LIVING

TERRACE

DINING

2

KITCH

3

TERRACE

CLOS

BEDROOM BEDROOM CL

HALL

HALL

LAV BATH

BEDROOM

GARDEN

UP

UP

GARAGE

LAUNDRY

ENT

FIRST FLOOR

DOWN

WALK

ROAD

WALK

1

N · S

LINE

SECOND FLOOR

MAID

CL

CLOS

DOWN

HALL

BATH

STORAGE

Location .. **HIGHLAND PARK, ILLINOIS**
Architect .. **L. MORGAN YOST**
Owners .. **THE MAURICE WEIGLES**

The use of split levels makes it possible to pack a lot of house on a 60 ft. lot. In the two-story portion that faces the road are concentrated the service facilities, with half-flights up to the maid's room and down to the garage. This leaves the rest of the house to work like a one-story design, with horizontal traffic in main living area.

Though the lot is narrow, it is deep, and the back of the house with its terraces faces ample garden and play space. Privacy is assured by the wing to the right, which blocks the view from street.

END

81

(3) The southern sun warms this sheltered rear terrace, gives it almost year-round usability—a planning point to remember in northern states.

CORNER LOTS CAN BE A BANE—OR A BOON

Location . . . . HOUSTON, TEXAS
Architect . . . . THOMPSON McCLEARY
Owners . . . . THE THOMPSON McCLEARYS

In most cities, corner lots draw a premium price. Their two-street position permits a freedom in planning the house. Service and main entrances can be separated. The line to city utilities is usually shorter, and there is only one neighbor.

However, there may be traffic on three sides, and the problem of calculating privacy on a corner lot is a real one.

The McClearys chose to back away from one busy street, even add a decorative brick wall for further seclusion. Their outdoor living porch with barbecue pit is screened—proof against curious eyes and insects.

The interior is designed flexibly for big or little entertaining, and to handle the changing needs of two boys.

(2) Motif of outdoor sheltering brick wall is repeated on interior masonry of fireplace chimney stack.

82

(3) Wall defines private area. (Photo taken above normal eye level to reveal more of house.) Liberal annual rainfall is recognized in design with wide overhangs, awning-type windows, inside barbecue, undercover access.

(1) Driveway is on quiet side street, with service entrance through carport to left. Main entrance, right.

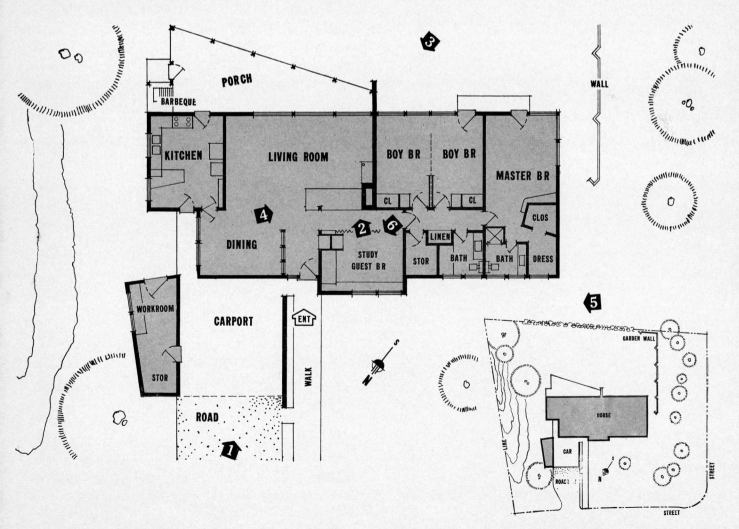

83

(4) Open planning that unites study, living and dining rooms helped win a Medal of Honor for this compact house in the A.I.A. Houston competition.

(5) Blank wall, softened by evergreens, faces street with heavy traffic.

(6) Opposite. Draperies open or close off study, which doubles as guest bedroom, with handy closet. This detail contains remodeling ideas for anyone's top floor—as an expansion room for a studious teen-ager, a home office for husband or wife, extra space for visiting family who stay a while. The McCleary boys have twin rooms that can be separated with a sliding door.

84

PRIVACY DESIRED, EVEN WITH NICE NEIGHBORS

Location . . . . **GLENDALE, MISSOURI**
near **ST. LOUIS**

Architects . . . **WEDEMEYER & HECKER**

Owners . . . . **THE EDWIN SHANNONS**

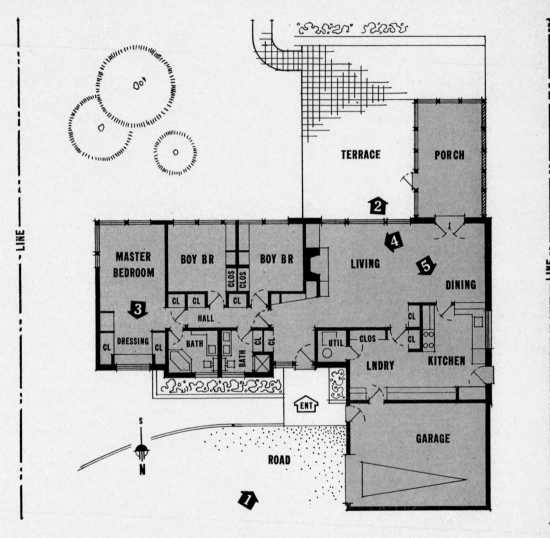

When the Shannons built their house, there was a vacant lot on each side. Soon after they moved in, two new houses went up beside them. This wasn't according to the original scheme, but they handled the matter directly. Up went a tall, handsome louvered fence, finished in the same grayed stain as the house, and the porch was screened on three sides.

It wasn't that the Shannons didn't like neighbors—but they cherish the freedom of living outdoors, even in the city. A bricked terrace for barbecues, garden beds stepped down with railroad ties, and low stone walls are as much a part of the architecture as the house itself. The terrace faces south, and the living room opens towards it. On the entrance side, only the high windows of baths and dressing room look out on the road.

The Shannons have two boys, eighteen and twenty-two. The size of the house is just right for a family at this stage. Not too big—but big enough to handle visiting grandchildren later on. Kitchen is generous. And count the closets!

(1) Approach, backed by trees and flanked by low evergreens that need no tending, is pleasant, but reveals little of the house. Service entrance through garage shares driveway.

(2) High fence is above eye-level of neighbors, permits private family fun on rear terrace. View through living room picture window.

(3) The mechanics of dressing are made easy for the Shannons with clothes storage built to their needs. Particular delight of Mrs. Shannon is a make-up table with running water and natural light. This is not too great a luxury, as lavatory is adjacent to bathroom plumbing, and a few feet of piping makes it possible. It maintains family harmony over bathroom occupancy.

(5) Clever detail in dining area is good device for remodeling, too. Buffet was ordered unfinished from well-known furniture manufacturer, stained to match mahogany woodwork. Step two is opposite.

(4) Dropped ceiling runs from entrance hall across left wall of living room to accentuate true room height and provide cove for indirect lighting. Note asymmetric fireplace, shallow mantel, and balancing composition above. Dining area is behind camera. Windows face terrace.

(5) Over buffet, sliding panels were installed to serve counter and cabinet. Hardboard panels are covered with grass cloth wallpaper. Result: buffet has furniture quality, built-in looks and function.

END

CLEVER DESIGN

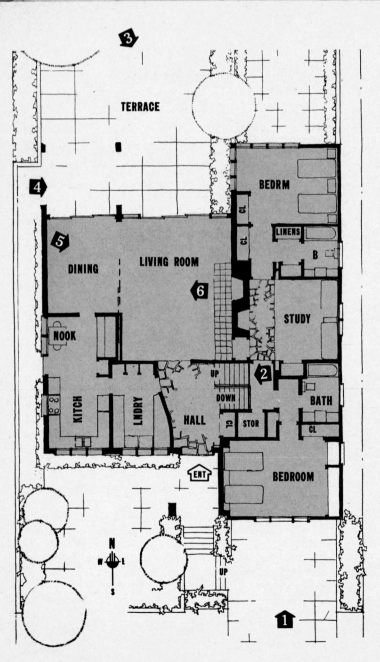

TERRACE

BEDRM

CL
CL
CL

LINENS

B

LIVING ROOM

DINING

STUDY

NOOK

UP

DOWN

BATH

KITCH

LNDRY

HALL

CL

STOR

CL

ENT

BEDROOM

N
W · E
S

UP

Location . . . . SEATTLE, WASHINGTON
Architects . . . WM. BAIN & H. OVERTURF
Owners . . . . THE DAVID BAINS

Given: a deep lot, only 60 ft. wide. No rear access, and irregular ground.

The land itself helped solve the desires of the owners. They wanted a compact plan, but not a two-story one. The result is a house with three levels, easing into each other with half-flights of stairs. All fits neatly on the ups and downs of the difficult site.

The hall is the hub of the house, on the middle level, as are the living and dining rooms, the kitchen and laundry. The top level contains bedrooms and study, which doubles as bedroom for guests. The steps down from the hall lead to recreation room, garage and maid's room and bath. Above (1), shows how the three levels integrate on the entrance side. Daughter's bedroom faces front.

On the private side of the house, two terraces permit communal or separate adult and adolescent entertaining.

SOLVES THE PROBLEM OF A NARROW UNEVEN LOT

(3) Above, rear view reveals three levels. Top terrace is for family or adults only. Lower terrace, down a few steps, leads off the recreation room, where the teen-age daughter entertains her friends. Privacy on a narrow lot (note peak of house next door) is assured by closing up the sides of the house, as plan shows, and installing a high fence.

(4) Detail of top terrace. Sliding doors open up living and dining rooms to sheltered area, which is pleasant through Seattle's short-lived but frequent showers. Windows of master bedroom overlook terraces. Note fence that steps down with the land.

(2) Entrance hall leads to living room at right. Curved wall of birch half-rounds conceals door to kitchen.

END

Living room, above (5), and dining room, below (6), can be one room—or two—with a modern version of Victorian sliding parlor doors. When doors are open, the "dining" room becomes a game room to augment hospitality, as shown. Or a table for three—the family. For more, the table behind the couch moves over to meet and match the standing one. Restraint in decoration and furnishings, plant arrangements reflect the Oriental influence, typical of the West Coast.

Houses for Irregular Land

There are three things to say for the "impossible site". It is often priced at a bargain. It is available when level lots have long been sold. A house built successfully on it is apt to have a touch of magic—in the view, or in the imagination of the design that made a structure even possible.

No house fitted against the contours of the land can be called conventional. Each one solves its special problem. The entry and garage may be on an upper level, with living below—or the other way around. Cost for a several-level house is more, but this should be balanced against the cost of the land, and the final stimulating results.

AN AERIAL PERCH GIVES DRAMA TO A TINY HOUSE

Location . . . . **SAN RAFAEL, CALIFORNIA**
Architect . . . . **FRED LANGHORST**
Owner . . . . . **ELIZABETH McCLAVE**

High places frighten some people, elate others. Miss McClave's house is literally standing on its toes at the peak of a hill. The panorama equals any airplane view.

The perch of the house is accomplished by ingenious structural engineering. While the V-supports are expensive, the total cost compared to carving out a level spot on the hill and shoring up the bank comes out about the same. The difference is the look of being poised, rather than settled.

For Miss McClave, a business woman, this house is a relaxing week-end retreat. She wanted a maximum of undivided floor space, and a minimum of upkeep, indoors and out. There are no weeds to pull on the sun-deck. The house is open for informal entertaining. Curtains draw across the accommodations for over-night guests.

(1) Footings anchor structural frame to crest of hill.

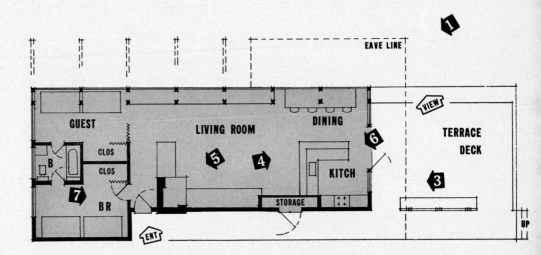

House is essentially one large room and a bedroom. Alcove can be closed off with a curtain for over-night guests—opened to enlarge living room for large parties.

(2) Entrance is on uphill side. Clerestory windows are angled to catch the most light from this direction. Ordinary windows would be in shadow of the hill. Redwood siding on exterior.

(3) Open deck is spectacular—day or night. In fine weather, most meals are served outside. Kitchen is convenient to deck, to indoor dining area and to living room, for refreshments.

(4) The bones of the house make a decorative V-pattern, looking toward the deck from living room. They are left uncovered to permit the most view. Bookshelf conceals kitchen corner.

98

(6) Neat as a ship's galley is this tiny, but efficient kitchen. Chest-high counter camouflages preparations, but lets hostess enjoy guests.

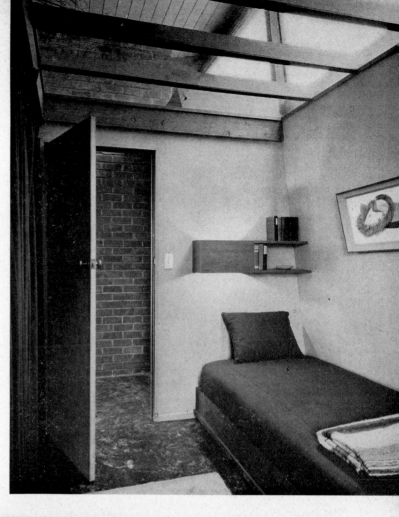

(7) Owner's bedroom shares clerestory, has another private outlook of its own. Second bunk is foot-to-foot with this one. Curtains pull across closet. In a week-end house, storage facilities can be minimal.

(5) Below, entertainment center for the chill seasons. Ample seating space is compacted in small room. The back of the fireplace wall, extended with counter back of couch, forms entrance hall.

99

END

ONE-LEVEL LIVING ON TWO-LEVEL LAND

Location . . . . WESTGATE, MARYLAND
        near WASHINGTON, D. C.

Architect. . . . WILLIAM SUITE

Owners . . . . THE WILLIAM SUITES

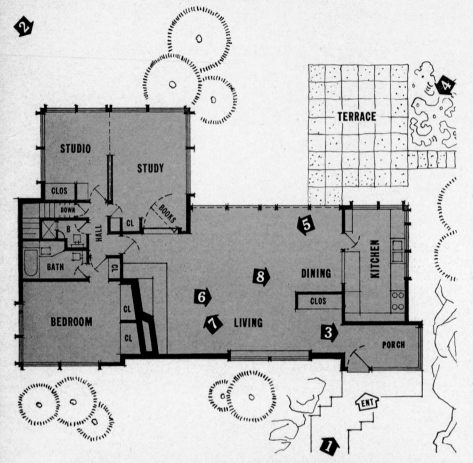

William and Loris Suite had trouble doubled. They both needed office space at home, since they are partners in design work. The architect-owner was wise enough to know that a house built to such special requirements might not be easily saleable, should working locale change.

The offices, therefore, are easily converted into bedrooms, or extra entertaining space depending upon the moment. If this seems sleight-of-hand, it is. Anyone who might live in the house later will be just as intrigued as those who visit.

The land levels made complications. The Suites wanted the convenience of a one-story plan. Garage and utility room fit nicely below. On a site as starkly rocky as any in New England, these designers used their advantages. Rocks can be beautiful, and look good all year round, whether one tends them or not.

100

(2) The one floor-living level shown on plan is distinguished by wood siding. Lower masonry section houses garage and utility rooms, entered from side street. Very little excavation was necessary—a real economy with rocky land.

(1) Charm of entrance is calculated. Staggered blocks in walk reflect rough contours of natural rock.

(3) Close-up of boulder through glass wall of entrance hall acts like a natural decorative mural. The site and indoor-outdoor design of house have all the character of a country home, although the location is a crowded suburb around Washington, D.C. Difficult land created the challenge—and yielded a bonus in its solution.

(4) Below, high ground is converted into terrace, links main living level with rise behind house. Sliding window-walls open up dining area to this private cove.

(5) Living end of spacious center room. Access to terrace at right. Loris Suite is a good complement to her architect husband. A skilled artist, she helps with his working drawings and renderings. When a joint project is under way, their separate offices can be opened into one large one. Mrs. Suite is also a designer of ceramics. Her kiln and clays occupy part of the generous garage.

(8) Left, dining corner can be formal with a quick flick of sliding doors to shut off signs of kitchen activity— or open and communal, as below.

104

Main theme behind planning is convertibility. For several reasons. Washington, D.C. is notably hot and humid during the summer. House can be opened fully to snare the slightest breeze. On grey, cool days, full draperies cover window-walls for a sense of comforting enclosure. (6) Large middle room is traffic center. Six-foot-high break holds coat closet.

(7) Legerdemain solves the double office problem. Above, fireplace corner is closed snug for entertaining. Below, pivoted bookshelves swing back, reveal architect's office. Sliding doors link this room with Mrs. Suite's studio. Both rooms can double as bedrooms for guests.

END

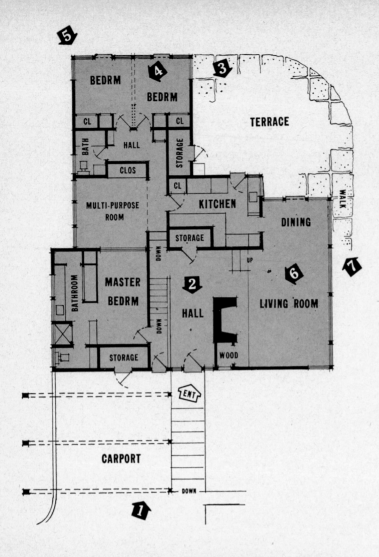

SLOPING ROAD CALLS FOR GARAGE TOP-SIDE

Location . . . . OAKLAND, CALIFORNIA
Architect . . . . ROGER LEE
Owners . . . . THE THOMAS LEAVERS

This house is surprisingly inexpensive, averaging ten dollars a square foot, including built-ins. Some ¾ in. birch was bought from an Air Force auction, some stones for the fireplace were hauled from the fields by the owners. The site said how the plan must be—and the house has ideas.

Since the road winds up the hill and the land slopes away, it was best economy to house the car above, fit the living space to the contours. The house divides naturally into two sections, separated by an old-fashioned amenity—a back hall. There is freedom for children on one side, for guests and parents on the other. Another nice detail is the many-use room just off the kitchen. Sliding doors permit it to be open or private. It triples as guest room, pleasant spot for sitter or nurse, and retreat for Mother while things are cooking.

(2) Entrance hall effects transition between high and low levels. Back of living room fireplace creates one wall—and vines in sunken plant bed cling to stones. Half-flight stairway is to bedroom. Glass surrounding flush entrance door admits ample light.

(1) Carport is just a few feet off uphill road. Main entrance is down the steps under shelter of roof overhang. Private entrance leads directly to top level and master bedroom—and to inside stairway down to living level.

(3) House steps down from high point of carport to lowest level of outdoor terraces. Paved area opposite is specially for adults, has direct access to kitchen, dining and living rooms. Closet opening to outdoors offers quick refuge for furniture.

CONTINUED, GARAGE TOP-SIDE

(4) Children's rooms can be one large play-room, or divided with sliding doors—note track. Dutch doors to room restrain small ones, but allow an open ear to activities. Twin built-in closets handle individual storage.

(5) Below, play yard for children is just outside their bedrooms. Within view of the adult terrace, it is psychologically separated with planting. Windows of master bedroom on upper level overlook this area.

(6) Living room is stepped down from entrance hall to follow slope of land. Ceiling is left high to simplify roof line—an economy device that lends extra drama. Novel room break: the spinet piano, with backing table. Location is perfect for a sangerfest or pianologue.

(7) Dining corner with sliding doors shares terrace—or links with living room when attention is on fireplace. Roll blinds cut sun when necessary.

END

DOCTOR'S HOUSE FITS GENTLY ROLLING LAND

Location . . . . BUCKS COUNTY, PENNSYLVANIA
Architect . . . . GEORGE DAUB
Owners . . . . THE DR. I. S. RAVDINS

Bucks County is famous for its famous residents. The divisions of land are generous, so there is no need to consider a community style. Some like Dutch Colonial, some like modern, but all seem to like the pastoral setting.

Dr. Ravdin holds the Chair of Surgery at the University of Pennsylvania Hospital. Although he currently lives near his work in Philadelphia, this house was built as his permanent home. The design evolved from the contours of the land, and the downhill long view. Here, too, the incoming road was high.

(3) A gentle rise of three steps to master bedroom is no hindrance to traffic on main living floor, but the lift in level permits full-height, light bedrooms on floor below.

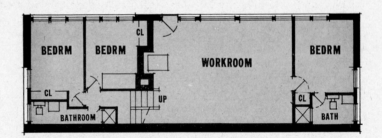

110

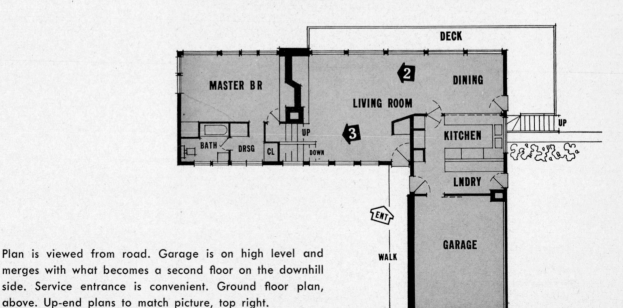

Plan is viewed from road. Garage is on high level and merges with what becomes a second floor on the downhill side. Service entrance is convenient. Ground floor plan, above. Up-end plans to match picture, top right.

(1) Living room is bounded with an open deck. Height accentuates long view across hills. Hobby workroom below.

(2) Dr. Ravdin's house is both rustic and sophisticated. For this subtlety, nice wood was blended with native stone. The exterior and most of the interior is of Philippine mahogany—also the custom-built television set to right of living room fireplace. Dining area behind camera.

111

END

AN ARTIST MAKES THE MOST OF VERMONT HILLS

Location . . . . **ARLINGTON, VERMONT**
Architects . . . **COWLES & KILEY**
Owners . . . . **THE JOHN ATHERTONS**

Mr. Atherton is an artist, a fisherman and a general lover of nature. He has recently written a book on trout fishing illustrated with his paintings.

Suitable background for his enthusiasms is his house on and in the midst of sizeable hills. The approach is deceptively modest, as he wished it, with the bulk of the structure invisible from the road. Both stories on the downhill side overlook exciting long views—including the Battenkill River, close enough for casting now and then.

Since Mr. A. works at home, his studio is isolated from the active part of the household. Kitchen and living room are on the lower level, near to porches and garden and river. The Athertons' daughter shares family talent, is studying music in college.

(1) Skylighted entrance spells character of house.

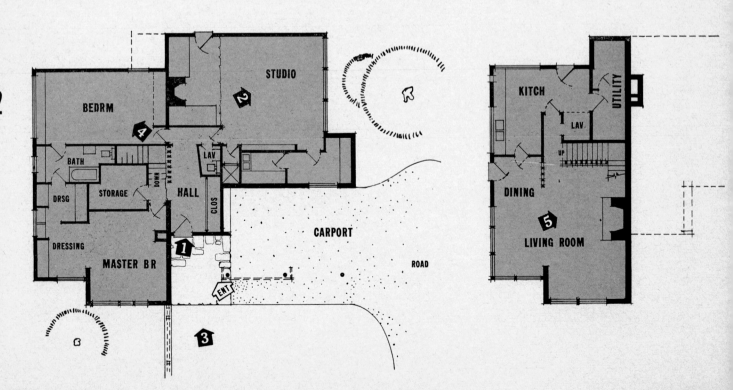

(2) Quiet studio has a fireplace of its own, bunk space for owner's relaxing, or for sleep-in guests. Ample closet contains artist's files and sink for washing brushes.

(3) Photo below matches plans—read them together. Road, right. Entrance, center. Upper bedroom level, left plan. Lower living and utility level, right plan.

(4) Daughter Mary's room shares the top-story view, has built-in desk.

(5) Ground floor living room accents comfort and personal expression.

114

SPECIFIED: BEDROOMS ON THE SECOND FLOOR

Location . . . . HANOVER, NEW HAMPSHIRE
Architects . . . E. H. & M. K. HUNTER
Owners . . . . THE Dr. O. SHERWIN STAPLES

Some people just prefer to sleep on a second story, and so with the Staples. Perhaps because Mrs. Staples is deeply southern. This worked out well with the hillsite and delivered a planned extra: due to the hills and thick hemlocks, the latest sun of the day is caught on the top deck. The bedrooms have become delightful family sitting rooms. Entrance, (1) below, hits the two levels midway.

Dr. Staples is an orthopedic surgeon practicing at the Mary Hitchcock Clinic in Hanover. Daughter "Taffy" is six.

(1) Driveway leads gently up hill to entrance, carport, and garage-storage at right.

115

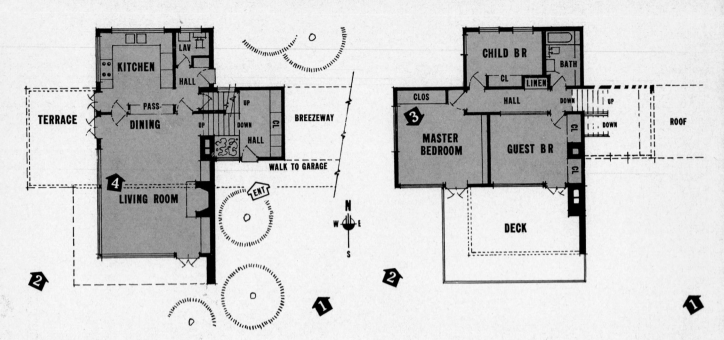

LOWER LEVEL. Entrance has half-flights up and down—is accessible to both levels. Lower living floor is a complete unit, well isolated from bedrooms above.

UPPER LEVEL. Completely a bedroom floor, it also offers an open deck with private sunning space, for owners or guests. The Doctor likes to relax here.

(4) Living and dining room opens on lower terrace, have a fine flexibility for easy serving. Entrance by stairs.

House is one of a five-part community project to develop raw hills just outside of town. Cost of land was $325 instead of $3,000 an acre. Utilities were brought in on petition. Houses had to be adapted to irregular land, light, and rough climate. (2) Above, master bedroom and deck open to south and west. (3) Below, bedroom with view of deck and hemlocks.

END

FIRST STAGE OF A HOUSE THAT IS STILL GROWING

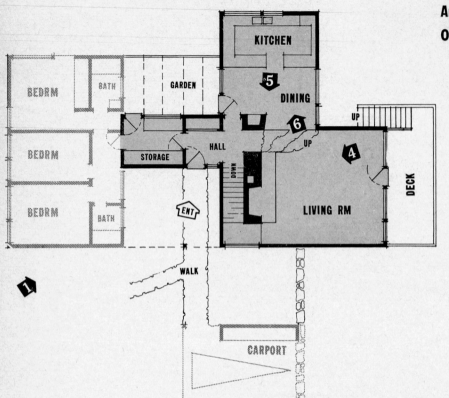

Location . . . . **LINCOLN, MASSACHUSETTS**
Architect . . . . **HUGH STUBBINS, JR.**
Owners . . . . **THE WILLIAM J. McCUNES, JR.**

An engineer and his wife found a wooded site and staked out futures. The grey on the plan shows the present house. The shaded lines mean what is to come. For now, the living is good. But a goal is defined. And expansion possibilities are built in—for a larger family.

There is just one child. The ground level with bath facilities does for a bedroom. Final role: playroom, shop and dark-room.

Heart of the house is a core of two fireplaces with natural steps between. This links several levels and rooms.

(1) Rear of house is unfinished. Portion that juts out will eventually be a hall to bedroom wing—now is a tiny bedroom, itself.

118

(2) Top deck leads off living room. Lower level, now for bedrooms, will provide dressing space for swimmers.

(3) Side view shows two-level character of house. Living level is above, with outside terrace under lattice for informal dining. Large kitchen window lights inner rooms.

(4) Living room looks larger than it is, because of open planning. Behind fireplace wall is stairway to lower level, with two-story window. Entrance is in hall, right background. Door opens to later bedroom wing. Curving steps also lead, right, to dining room and kitchen. Deck extends look of living room at opposite end.

(5) Dining room fireplace is twin to one in living room, beyond. It forms a visual, but not a real break between hall, living and dining rooms. This allows easy circulation for many guests—or much family.

Because the McCune house is deep in the woods, well beyond the town water mains of Lincoln, it has been made as fireproof as possible. Walls are cinder block, exposed inside and out—and painted. Floors are concrete and slate flagstone. Roof is built-up pitch and gravel. (6) The sunny kitchen merges with dining area, which steps down to living room. Fireplace with side table is a real indoor barbecue.

121

END

UNUSUAL MEETING OF INDIANA DUNES AND STRUCTURE

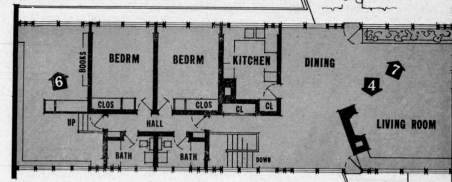

Location . . . . **DUNES ACRES, INDIANA**
Architects . . . **GEORGE FRED & WILLIAM KECK**
Associates . . . **ROBERT B. TAGUE, WILLIAM REED**
Owners . . . . **THE PROF. AVERY CRAVENS**

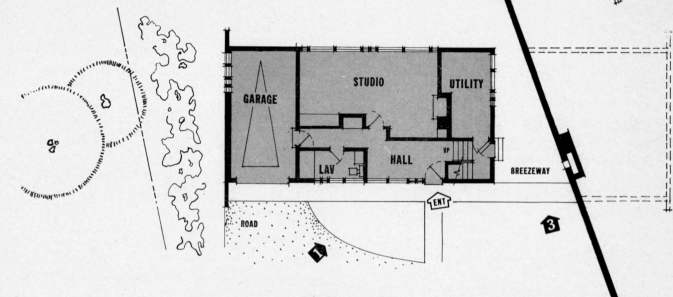

(1) Entrance view below illustrates lower plan. Retaining wall breaks levels. Plans match.

(2) Rear of house is open. Living room to left meets natural ground. Bedrooms to right top ground floor rooms. Walk leads up from underpass. The rest of the land is for play.

Professor Craven teaches history at the University of Chicago, and is now on a scholar's trip to England. Retirement time will be coming up soon, but his study is ready for new writings and research.

The house takes the dunes as they are, and settles down comfortably with the main living on the upper floor. For ease, a path cleaves the lower level. The beach is nearby, and a generous ground-floor lavatory has a shower for bathers. Windows are fixed, and louver ventilators are openable at will. This has a special value, when the wind blows the fine dune sand.

Mrs. Craven paints in her studio on the ground floor. (See plan.) She is from Georgia, and sentimental. Her favorite possessions are around her, as they should be, in such a personal house.

(3) Pass-through on entrance side has extra function— service deliveries are handy at lower level door. Walk for guests leads to dining room.

CONTINUED,
STRUCTURE FOR INDIANA DUNES

(4) Structural materials make honest decoration, offer a simple background for pet collected items. Fireplace face is of painted concrete block, and chimney acts as room break. Fireplace itself is unobtrusive, but available, with tongs and antique woodbox.

(5) Architect Keck was an original designer of the solar house, utilizing the sun's heat. Therefore, it is not too unusual that he walls a house with glass, in Indiana, facing south. Glass is fixed, which is economical. Ventilation is through controllable louvers.

(6) Professor's study has outlook over grounds. Research material is stowed in cabinets at right. The family feeling for old things prevails. Cabinets, left background, really "open the windows."

(7) Mrs. Craven enjoys her tea and game table by the dining-room plant box. This again, is a happy mixture of the precious past with the new.

END

They Knew What They Wanted

Behind everyone's work lies the ideal of living the best way, eventually. What "best" means is an individual matter. It may be based on sentiment and years-old dreams. Or on the pride of ownership. Or on convenience, to diminish the mechanics of a house and accentuate what goes on inside. Or a combination of all three.

Each house in this chapter tells an individual story of good living, made-to-order. Budget was not a major matter, but special desires were. All of the owners have experienced owning a home or two before, so their opinions are educated. Taste, firmed with strong family ties, can be transplanted. It is none the less a conviction, wherever it shows. Or taste can be brand new.

AN ARCHITECT'S NEW HOUSE MEETS THE TIMES

William Bain has designed his own house before. The three Bain children grew up in a large house with a view of the water and expansive well-kept gardens. Now, the two boys are launched. They return often to visit, and aim to continue when they have their own families. The youngest daughter is just starting her teens.

Mrs. Bain took a good look around and decided it was time to consolidate. Help was becoming harder and harder to find, both for inside and outside work.

The Bains' new house can be small enough for three—or can be opened to handle anything short of a regiment. Planting is concentrated, Oriental-fashion in small, easily-tended beds. The rest of the area is paved. A maid and a gardener one day a week are all the help required.

128

Location . . . . SEATTLE, WASHINGTON
Architects . . . WILLIAM BAIN & HARRISON OVERTURF
Owners . . . . THE WILLIAM BAINS

(2) Approach is paved for parking. Detail (1), top of page.

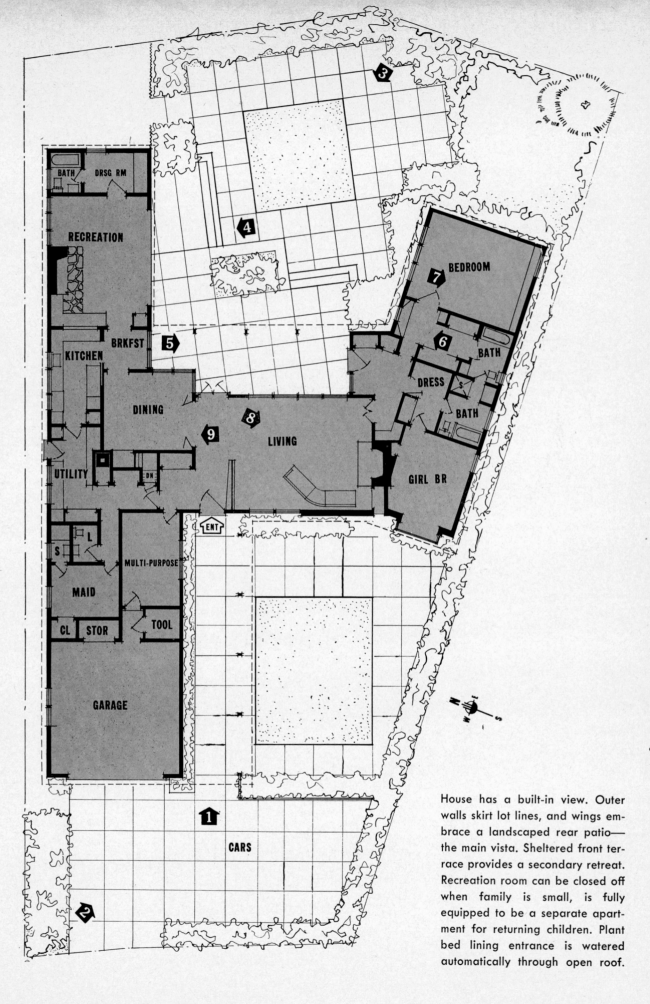

BATH
DRSG RM

RECREATION

BRKFST

KITCHEN

DINING

UTILITY

DN

MAID

S
L
CL
STOR
TOOL

MULTI-PURPOSE

GARAGE

ENT

CARS

LIVING

9

8

5

4

3

7
BEDROOM

6
BATH

DRESS
S

BATH

GIRL BR

1

2

129

House has a built-in view. Outer walls skirt lot lines, and wings embrace a landscaped rear patio—the main vista. Sheltered front terrace provides a secondary retreat. Recreation room can be closed off when family is small, is fully equipped to be a separate apartment for returning children. Plant bed lining entrance is watered automatically through open roof.

(3) Square of lawn is soft for sunning, can be mowed quickly; walks swept. Weeding is simple in confined plant beds. Personnel: daughter Nancy and friend.

(4) Recreation room, as seen from the patio. Dancers shuttle between cork floor and concrete under a night sky. High jog in fireplace is barbecue center. At left is pass-door to kitchen—for help-yourself service. When the sons live in, the couches pull out to become full beds. On their first Christmas homecoming in the new house, the boys invited 150 friends—and entertained 258. (Friends had married.) The house and grounds took it very easily.

131

For contemplative moments or just plain relaxing, this open lanai is favored. It faces the patio and gardens beyond (opposite page). Translucent roof transfers soft light, keeps off rain. Living room is behind wall of windows. (5)

(6) Both mother and daughter have dressing rooms. Vanity with triple mirrors belongs to Mrs. Bain. Natural light comes through shadow box. Bedroom wing has its own furnace with bedside control, as well as separate hot water—insuring steady and quick service to outlying section of house.

(7) Master bedroom. Rounded contours and rich textures soften straightforward architecture with sentiment.

(8) Living room bridges two halves of house. Oriental flavor in decoration is expressed in lines of furniture, low tables, accessories and plant arrangements. Couch angled to permit two views at once —of fire and patio.

(9) Dining room can seat ten or accommodate sixty for a buffet supper. Louvered folding doors close off preparations—or open up space completely to link with living room and play area.

END

CHOICE POSSESSIONS ADD TO GOOD LIVING IN A MODIFIED MODERN HOUSE

The Hudgins have been busy going places most of their lives. Interesting years in many parts of the United States and abroad, and living in a succession of other people's houses convinced them of one thing. They wanted a home of their own. They had collected furniture and objects with special meanings of memory. These needed a home, too.

One of the requirements was a beautiful natural setting and a house that made the most of it. Ravines border two sides of the site, a lake is to the rear. In Texas, it is important to orient the house to the breezes and take care with the sun. Even with the large glass area that faces the interior gardens, the house is so placed to be completely comfortable. The alliance of traditional furnishings with a modern feeling in plan and details has been accomplished with great harmony.

Location . . . . **HOUSTON, TEXAS**
Architect . . . . **HAMILTON BROWN**
Owners . . . . **THE T. F. HUDGINS**

(2) Richness of furnishings through house is keynoted at entrance. Architecture has clean, simple lines, tempered with a suggestion of traditional paneling to reflect flavor of decoration. Couch faces fireplace.

(1) Magnificent trees line entrance drive. Garage and service entry to left. Gabled roof is traditional touch.

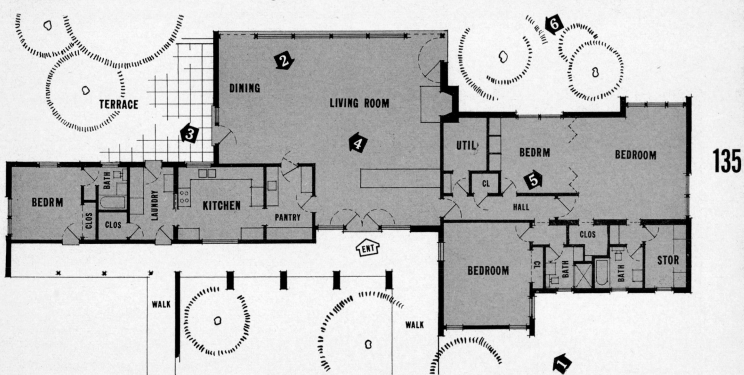

TERRACE

DINING

LIVING ROOM

BEDRM

BATH

CLOS

CLOS

LAUNDRY

KITCHEN

PANTRY

ENT

UTIL

CL

BEDRM

BEDROOM

HALL

CLOS

BEDROOM

CL

BATH

BATH

STOR

WALK

WALK

135

CONTINUED, CHOICE POSSESSIONS ADD TO GOOD LIVING

(3) Left, the one-floor plan lends itself to easy indoor-outdoor living. Down a stone step from the dining room (and just outside the kitchen) is a paved terrace for pleasant meals under the shade trees. (4) Below, open feeling in dining room is sustained by slim-scaled chairs and table, which do not block view. Cherished Oriental screen is used architecturally on buffet wall to link large windows. Openable shutters in two decks permit flexible control of light and sun.

(5) Sentiment is teamed with function in twin master bedrooms, divisible with louvered doors. Light colors look cool, set off the fine dark woods in family furniture.

(6) The open side, or "rear" of the house faces private grounds, terminated by a lake.

END

HOSPITALITY HOUSE — WITH AMENITIES BUILT IN

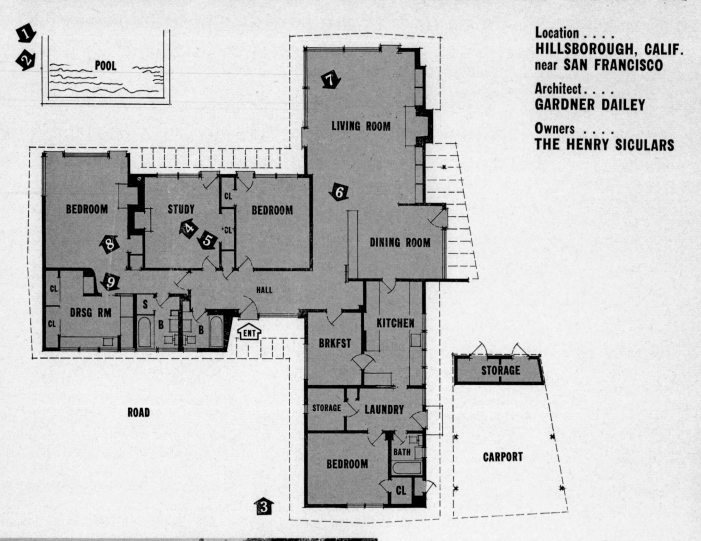

Location . . . .
HILLSBOROUGH, CALIF.
near SAN FRANCISCO

Architect . . . .
GARDNER DAILEY

Owners . . . .
THE HENRY SICULARS

POOL

LIVING ROOM

BEDROOM   STUDY   BEDROOM

CL   CL

DINING ROOM

HALL

DRSG RM   S   B   B   KITCHEN

CL   CL   ENT   BRKFST

ROAD

STORAGE   LAUNDRY   STORAGE

BEDROOM   BATH   CARPORT

CL

138

It comes naturally to the Siculars to like people. Perhaps because of this, and the nature of Mr. Sicular's work, much of his business is transacted while he is a host.

For such a business and living program, a difficult site was chosen—one of the few undeveloped lots in a built-up suburb. The lot was available because it was a low area with a drainage problem, and had been a water supply for the neighborhood years back. A judicious use of drain tile solved this problem and a deep well was sunk. The swimming pool evolved as a bonus.

To make matters worse, the lot was bounded by roads on three sides. A good fence lets bathers, guests or owners, be themselves.

(1) Fence completely shields house and pool, is slotted for air circulation. (Photo was taken from above normal eye level to reveal house.)

(2) Business and personal friends of the Siculars compete with teen-age daughter and followers for use of the pool.

(3) Front of house is deceptively simple, practically windowless and serves as shield for the garden-pool side.

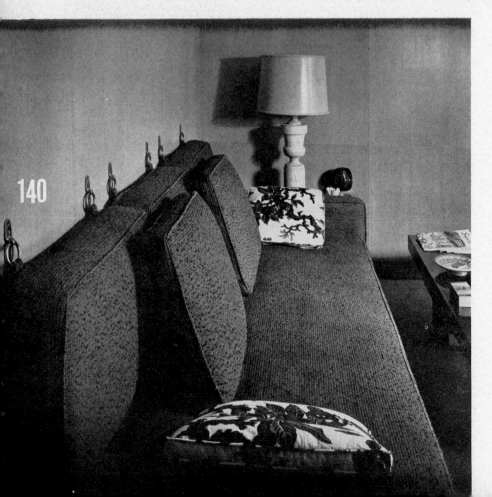

(4) Study is pleasant place for conferences when living room is filled with guests. It is an office for Mr. and Mrs. Sicular, has closet and cupboard on wall to right. Fireplace shares a common chimney with one in master bedroom.

(5) Left, couch in study wears its daytime look. When guests overflow, this room offers stand-by sleeping quarters. Back cushions are hooked onto wall for greater stability—never land on floor when couch is pulled out to become a bed.

140

(6) Built-in sideboard creates break between entrance and dining area. Snugly aligned chairs form a hall bench, are quickly available for extra seating. Television faces living room, can be camouflaged if it threatens the spirit of the party.

(7) Below, living room with television set closed. Built-in bar also disappears until needed. Fireplace has gas igniter to make a successful fire a casual matter. Window wall opposite fireplace looks out on pool.

(8) Master bedroom is a lounge in itself—a complete retreat. As with every other room in the house, some form of music or entertainment is built-in. A Degas print conceals a television set, viewable comfortably from the bed. The outlook on the pool shows bath-house.

(9) Dressing room for Mrs. Sicular makes the most of wall space with mirrors. High-up windows provide the necessary natural light, face entrance road. Cupboards are calculated for hats, shoes, lingerie. Make-up table has running water.

END

A NEW YORK EXECUTIVE TAKES TO THE SUN

Mr. Fred Eldean, public relations counsel, shuttles by plane between New York and Phoenix. Formerly the Eldeans lived East, in a large family house, filled with furnishings accumulated over the years. One look at the desert—and they decided on a new way of life. The old patterns were left behind completely. As much as possible, furniture is built in, for easy maintenance. The house accents informal living, which guests enjoy as much as the Eldeans.

Location . . . . SCOTTSDALE, ARIZONA
Architect . . . . BLAINE DRAKE
Owners . . . . THE FRED ELDEANS

143

(1) Sun porch can be open, top and sides—or protected with roll-up slat blinds when desert sun becomes too hot.

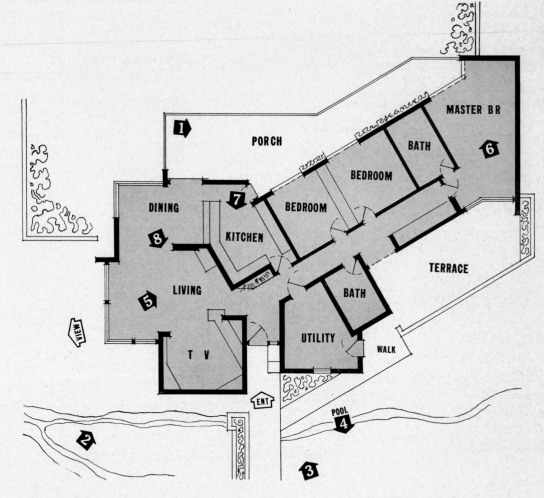

(2) Cactus and desert flowers bloom beside common varieties for a beauty in contrasts. Birds flock to foliage.

144

(3) Entrance. Glassed-in terrace to right overlooks lily pool, formed by cementing a natural gully. Exterior and interior wall material is native pumice block. "Easy to clean," says Mrs. Eldean. "Just rub off a spot with another piece of block." Its light color reflects heat.

(4) Cool pool defies desert aridity and is in demand for bathing or barbecues. (Two sons live in nearby Phoenix.) Shelter allows escape from the sun. Walks link pool to house and to extra guest house, adjoining garage. Other outbuilding is for deep well pump and shop.

(5) Fireplace in a wide-angled corner can be shared from any point in living or television rooms, yet does not dominate a major wall.

(6) Orientation of plan to view and sun results in interesting room shapes. Master bedroom has solid wall for privacy, opens onto porch. Right.

146

(7) Low ceilings harbor indirect lighting throughout. Kitchen emphasizes natural woods. Thermador oven utilizes "dead" corner.

147

(8) TV room is windowless. Right wall holds set, radio-phonograph, and movie screen. Decorating colors through house are muted, with natural block and pale yellow ceilings. Spark comes from dozens of bright or patterned pillows.

END

BUSINESS AND PLEASURE ARE BLENDED IN CALIFORNIA VALLEY

Location .... **MODESTO, CALIFORNIA**
Architect.... **GARDNER DAILEY**
Owners .... **A VINTNER AND FAMILY**

In the heart of a wine-growing valley in California lives the head of a well-known wine company. The heat of the valley is good for grapes, but sometimes stifling for people. The house is designed to accommodate. White tiles on the roof reflect the sun's heat. The house is set at right angles to the prevailing summer wind, so it becomes a breezeway when opened up. The owners use their house in a business way—sometimes entertaining lavishly. The husband purchased a real merry-go-round horse, and is so fond of it, it is kept in the living room, to the delight of the two small sons.

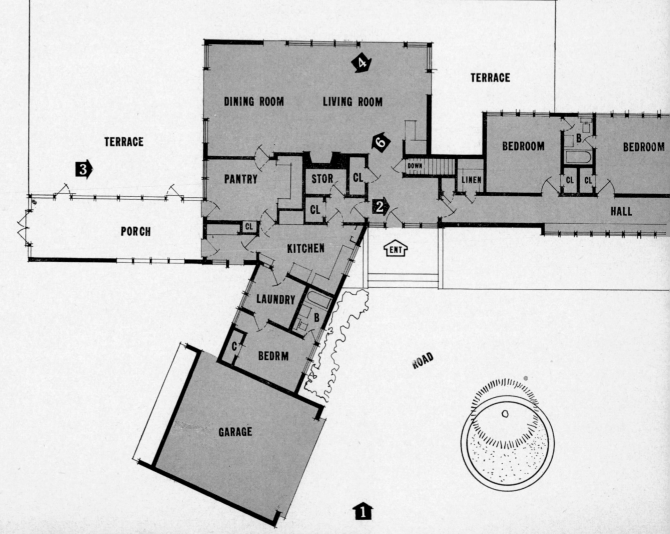

BATH

BEDROOM

DRSG

5

(1) Above. Single story rambling plan has true ranch-house feeling. One-room-wide wings encourage flow of air.

(2) Right, doors that control climate. Louvered shutters admit air, cut hot sun. Glass captures light, keeps out blowing sand on grey or windy day.

149

(3) Low green vineyards surround house. Eye-easing, they are a comforting reminder of the source of success, are used in part to experiment with new grape strains. Willows shade terrace off dining room.

(4) A business corner. Here executives and taste experts meet to study bouquet and body of wines for the market. Table folds up and door conceals supplies.

(5) Good bed, view and efficient storage key master bedroom. Door, left, to dressing room.

151

(6) Living-dining room is richly furnished to owners' taste. It opens to two terraces on opposing walls. Fireplace, left. Center windows look out on expansive lawn. Wine-testing station and rocking horse behind camera. Dining area at far end.

END

FUN AND CONVENIENCE ARE PART OF THIS DESIGN

Location .... **SHREVEPORT, LOUISIANA**

Architect .... **WILLIAM B. WIENER**

Owners .... **THE WILLIAM B. WIENERS**

There is much going on at the Wiener house with a teen-age son and daughter. The parents enjoy themselves, too. The house is divided into separate areas that can be shared or private, depending upon the circumstances. The living room opens onto a generous terrace. Game room has radio-phonograph, a good floor for dancing and adjacent refreshments. During an oversized youthful party, the parents can retreat to a master bedroom well-equipped for relaxing.

The lines of this house are clean, but behind the smooth wood panels, there are surprises. Every inch works.

(1) Entrance detail. Slotted overhang modifies sun on picture window. Supporting wall shields road side, leads to rear terrace.

(3) Terrace is secluded extension of living and game rooms. Brick wall, left, insulates bedroom area from party gaiety.

152

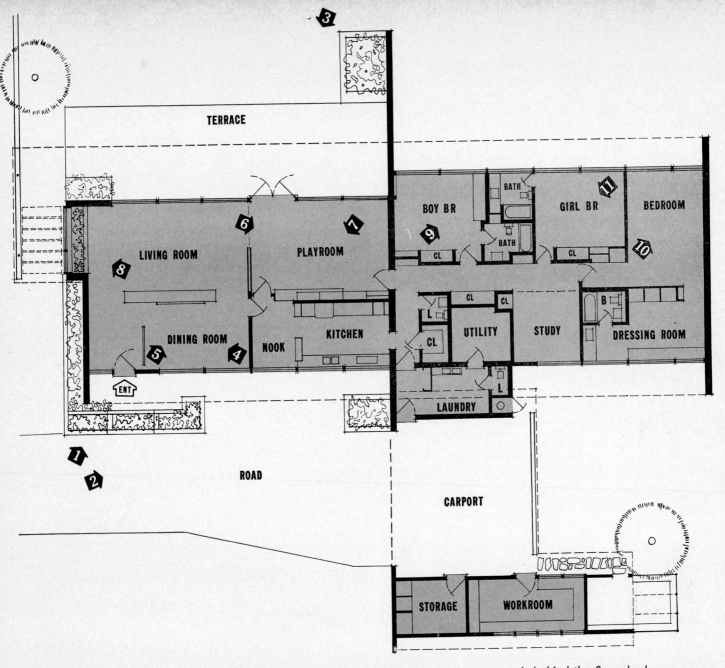

TERRACE

LIVING ROOM

8

DINING ROOM

5

ENT

1

2

ROAD

6

PLAYROOM

7

NOOK

4

KITCHEN

BOY BR

9

CL

BATH

BATH

UTILITY

CL

CL

L

CL

L

LAUNDRY

L

STUDY

GIRL BR

11

CL

BEDROOM

10

B

DRESSING ROOM

CARPORT

STORAGE

WORKROOM

3

(2) Driveway from main road enters carport with shop and storage to right. Main entrance is behind the flowerbeds.

153

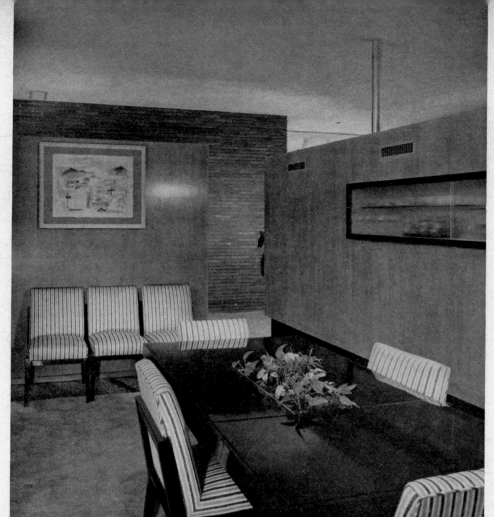

(4) Semi-partitions preserve open plan, but isolate dining room from entrance (far wall) and living room (right). Smooth walls make room seem larger.

154

(5) Detail of partition above. Flush cabinet doors conceal choice dining service. Drawers hold silver and trays. Sliding doors of ribbed glass keep glassware inconspicuous.

(6) Architect Wiener uses built-ins and play-proof materials to meet diverse requirements. Game-room can handle a highball and Haydn, beer and be-bop, cokes and cribbage—or any combination of same. Radio, phonograph and records behind cabinet doors in right wall. Buffet shelf is in rest position.

(7) For refreshments or food, shelf pulls out, kitchen pass-door slides open.

156

(8) Overhang tempers hot Louisiana sun and an indoor garden thrives behind picture window. Plant bed is focal point in room without a fireplace—and is self-decorating.

(9) The fancy for built-ins prevails through house. This is the boy's version, to his specifications. Engineered closets, twin beds complete the room. Door, right, leads to bath.

(10) Center. Master bedroom is equipped to be self-sufficient as a ship. Radio, lights, reading rack are reachable. Nearby dressing room has wall of closets, counter lavatory.

(11) Bottom. Girl's room has feminine nuances. Small drawers for little things are flanked by hanging closets. Desk is good-looking as well as efficient. Vanity table by twin beds.

END

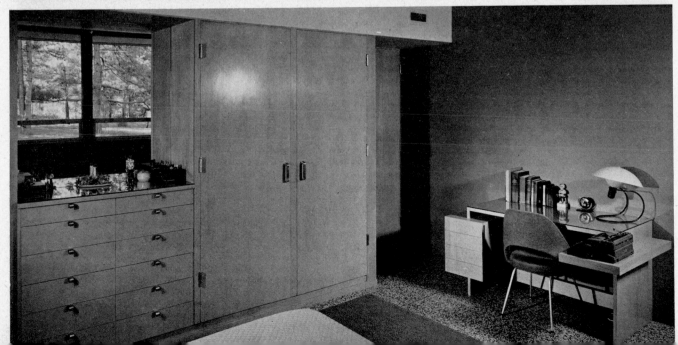

EASTERN TRADITION FLAVORS WESTERN PLAN

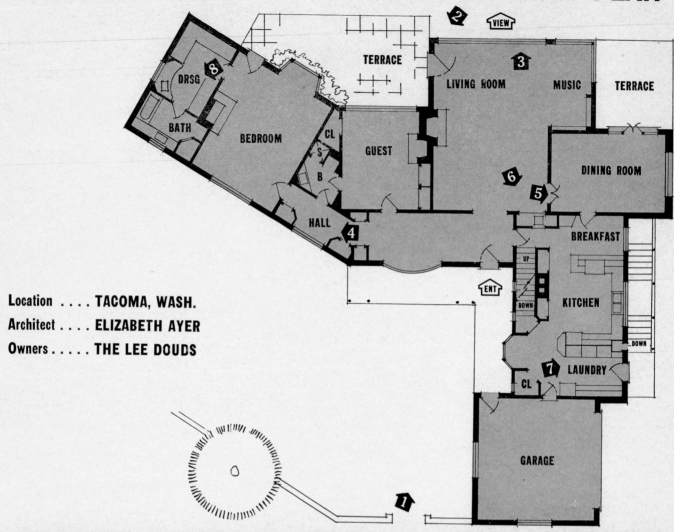

Location . . . . **TACOMA, WASH.**

Architect . . . . **ELIZABETH AYER**

Owners . . . . . **THE LEE DOUDS**

158

(1) Entrance. Typical of a western ranch-house is the rambling plan, patio with covered walk, weathered shingles and stone-work with spilled mortar. Colonial characteristics are white siding, shuttered paned windows, suggestion of a second story.

While their three children were growing up, the Douds collected desires here and there towards the house that would eventually include just the two elders.

These ideas were unrelated—details admired in houses of friends, an affection for high, beamed ceilings and a leaning towards a traditional flavor. But they also wanted a one-floor plan, the convenience of built-ins, and generous windows.

Mrs. Doud was willing to discard emotional convictions, if necessary, for function. The architect showed her how the two could be combined gracefully.

(2) Opposite page. Rear of house is modern in its free use of glass in living room.

(3) Right. View of lake and private grounds reveals the reason behind window wall.

159

(4) Built-in hall cabinets have modern function, but make a bow to the past. Period silver pieces look at home with muntined window and paneled doors.

(5) Dining room was adapted from one admired earlier. Wallpaper mural and dark ceiling contrast sharply with white brick walls. Pattern camouflages kitchen door.

The Douds have filled their house with little details that have a special meaning or serve a special need.

(6) Right. Corner in living room to make host happy is complete with sink and refrigerator. Folding doors pull across nook—to look just like paneled wall.

(8) Below. Curved lines of vanity are graceful, allow maximum space in passageway to bathroom beyond.

(7) Above. Laundry is separate from kitchen, but sliding panel establishes communication. Services fit neatly into back entry hall—a good device for remodeling.

END

(2) Radiant heat of the sun at Denver's high altitude keeps plants blooming all winter in glassed-in garden.

A HOUSE THAT EVERYONE LIVES IN — YEAR-ROUND

Location . . . . DENVER, COLORADO
Architect . . . . VICTOR HORNBEIN
Owners . . . . THE VICTOR HORNBEINS

This could be called a 24-hour-a-day house, since the owner-architect has his office at home—and his family and fun. It is also a four-season house. A garden and terrace, including a shade tree, are within the exterior walls. When a blizzard descends from the mountains upon Denver, the Hornbeins still have greenery around them. Part of the success in mixing many types of activity in a relatively small house is an irregular plan that contains a new interest behind each jog.

(3) Formidable look from road belies easy living inside. Right wall shields indoor court, fence confines play yard.

An imaginative use of brick and wood is a trademark with architect Hornbein, and is no better displayed than in his own house. Bold overhang forms sheltered walk to entrance (1); slots admit light and rain to plant bed beneath. Plan shows how the out-of-doors is integrated closely with the structure. Office is isolated, has a covered walk to house, an outside path for business visitors.

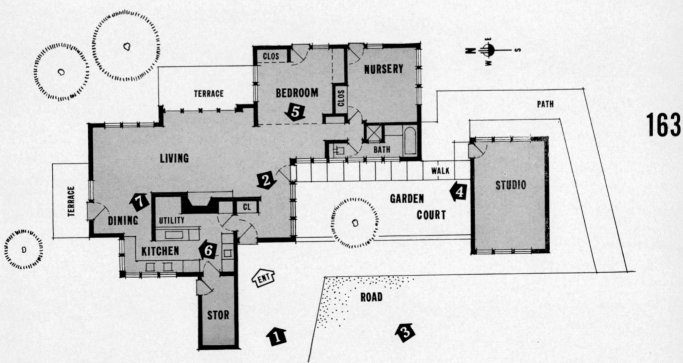

163

CONTINUED, YEAR-ROUND HOUSE

(4) Denver can be hot in the summer. Mr. and Mrs. Hornbein relax in the shade of their own indoor tree. Open roof gives partial sun control, lets rain water plants.

(5) Skylighted entrance hall eases into living room. Ample couch in front of fireplace furnishes double bed space for guests. Note interior use of brick and wood. View from bedroom.

(6) Warm woods, red brick, touches of copper contrast with cool stainless steel to make a kitchen guests want to visit. Pullman style, it rounds brick wall to merge with dining area.

(7) Just beyond dining table is music and cocktail corner. Low ceiling evokes intimate atmosphere, creates visual break with high-ceilinged center of living room, extending right.

END

CONCORDANCE

A Guide to Details

Concordance

Kitchens

Music Rooms

CONTINUED, CONCORDANCE

Roofs

170

Vacation Houses

Regional Distribution Directory

171

INDEX
to
Owners

Our thanks first to the owners for their infectious enthusiasm. They had the dreams. Credit next to the architects, who converted desires into substance for living. And third, to the architectural photographers, who make house reporting possible.

172

Architects

Photographers